THE GREAT LAKES

An Environmental Atlas and Resource Book

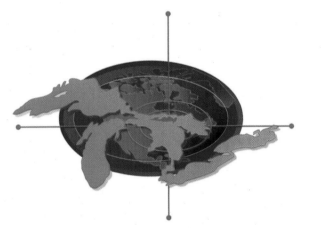

Jointly produced by:

Government of Canada
Toronto, Ontario
and

United States Environmental Protection Agency
Great Lakes National Program Office
Chicago, Illinois

Third Edition
1995
Reprinted 2002

Acknowledgements

The third edition of this atlas consists of a revision and update of the original document produced by Environment Canada, United States Environmental Protection Agency and authored by Lee Botts and Bruce Krushelnicki. Six maps originally produced by Brock University Cartography Group have been retained in this revised edition. The high quality cartography was recognized by the British Cartographical Society and received an award for excellence in cartography and design in 1988.

Contributors to the third edition:

Principal editors:

Kent Fuller,
United States Environmental
Protection Agency,
Great Lakes National Program Office

Harvey Shear, Ph.D.,
Jennifer Wittig,
Environment Canada,
Ontario Region

The following people and agencies have given valuable assistance to this project by providing information, reviewing or contributing to text, or by making helpful comments for this third edition:

W. Adam, Great Lakes Commission, Ann Arbor, Michigan

S. Barrett, Waterfront Regeneration Trust, Toronto, Ontario

M. Evans, Environment Canada, Ontario Region, Toronto, Ontario

C. Flaherty, United States Environmental Protection Agency, Great Lakes National Program Office, Chicago, Illinois

P. Fong, Statistics Canada, Ottawa, Ontario

A. Gilman, Great Lakes Health Effects Program, Environmental Health Directorate, Health Canada, Ottawa, Ontario

V. Glumac, Environmental Conservation Branch, Environment Canada, Ontario Region, Burlington, Ontario

J. Hartig, Wayne State University, Detroit, Michigan

J. Mortimer, Great Lakes Health Effects Program, Environmental Health Directorate, Health Canada, Ottawa, Ontario

N. Patterson, Environment Canada, Ontario Region, Toronto, Ontario

N. Stadler-Salt, Environment Canada, Ontario Region, Burlington, Ontario

S. Thorp, Great Lakes Commission, Ann Arbor, Michigan

J. Tilt, Ontario Ministry of Natural Resources, Toronto, Ontario

M. Webb, Environment Canada, Ontario Region, Toronto, Ontario

Principal authors and contributors to the first and second editions:

R. Beltran, United States Environmental Protection Agency, Great Lakes National Program Office, Chicago, Illinois

L. Botts, Northwestern University, Evanston, Illinois (Author)

P. Brown, L. Gasparotto, A. Hughes, Brock University Cartography, St. Catharines, Ontario

T. Clarke, Environment Canada, Ontario Region, Burlington, Ontario

D. Cowell, Environment Canada, Ontario Region, Toronto, Ontario

K. Fuller, United States Environmental Protection Agency, Great Lakes National Program Office, Chicago, Illinois

B. Krushelnicki, Institute of Urban and Environmental Studies, Brock University, St. Catharines, Ontario (Author)

Additional contributors:

J. Anderson, Department of Geography, Concordia University, Montreal, Quebec

A. Ballert, Great Lakes Commission, Ann Arbor, Michigan

A. Beeton, Great Lakes Environmental Research Laboratory, NOAA, Ann Arbor, Michigan

F. Berkes, Institute of Urban and Environmental Studies, Brock University, St. Catharines, Ontario

M. Brooksbank, Environment Canada, Ontario Region, Toronto, Ontario

V. Cairns, Department of Fisheries and Oceans, Burlington, Ontario

D. Coleman, Inland Waters and Lands Directorate, Environment Canada, Ontario Region, Burlington, Ontario

M. Dickman, Department of Biological Sciences, Brock University, St. Catharines, Ontario

G. Francis, Department of Environment and Resource Studies, University of Waterloo, Waterloo, Ontario

A. Hamilton, International Joint Commission, Ottawa, Ontario

C. Herdendorf, Ohio Sea Grant, Put-In Bay, Ohio

S. Leppard, Land Use Research Associates, Toronto, Ontario

J. Lloydd, Environment Canada, Ontario Region, Burlington, Ontario

J. Middleton, Institute of Urban and Environmental Studies, Brock University, St. Catharines, Ontario

M. Neilson, Environmental Conservation Branch, Environment Canada, Ontario Region, Burlington, Ontario

G. Rodgers, National Water Research Institute, Environment Canada, Burlington, Ontario

R. Shipley, Welland Canal Preservation Association, St. Catharines, Ontario

W. Sonzogni, Wisconsin State Laboratory of Hygiene, University of Wisconsin, Madison, Wisconsin

J. Vallentyne, Department of Fisheries and Oceans, Burlington, Ontario

Contents

1

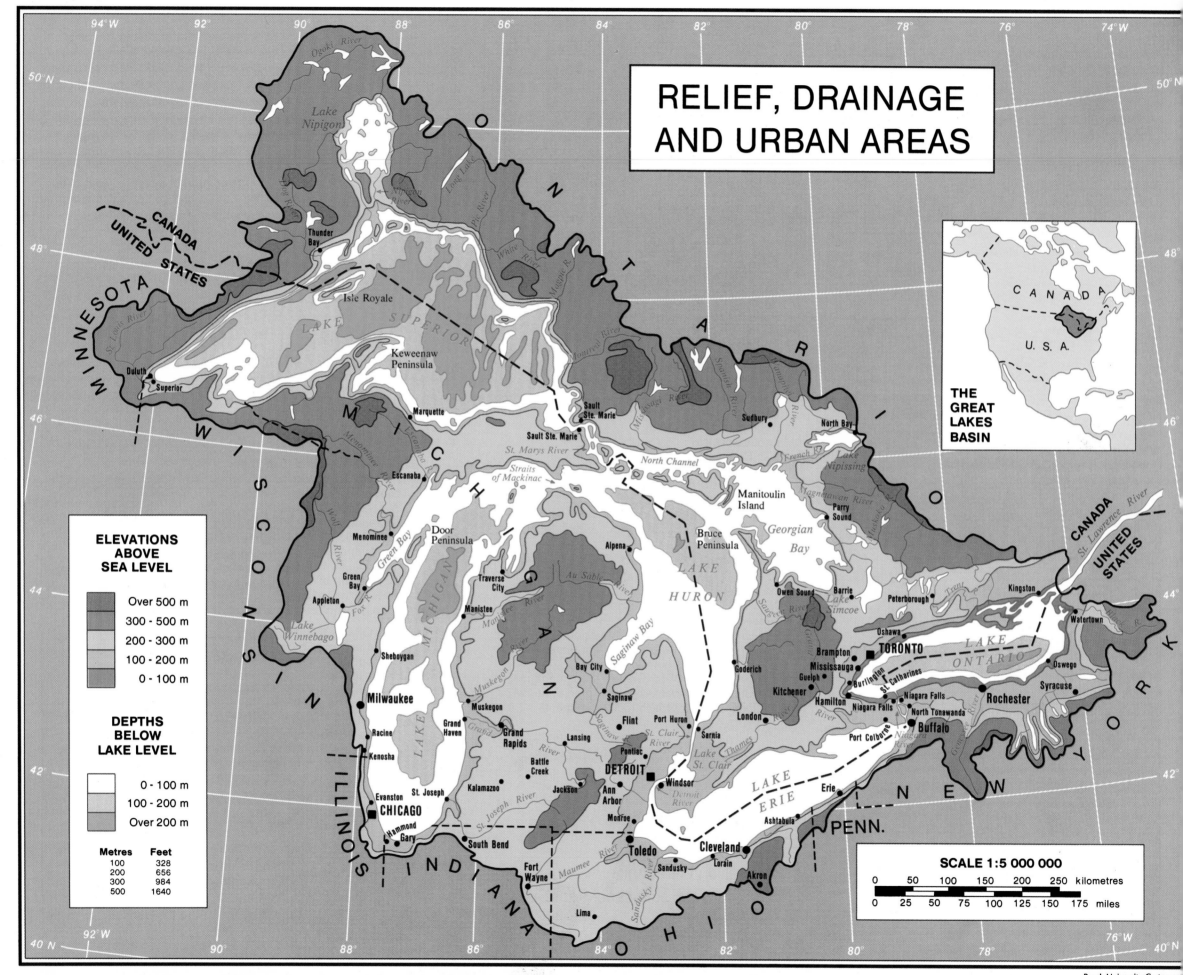

RELIEF, DRAINAGE AND URBAN AREAS

THE GREAT LAKES BASIN

ELEVATIONS ABOVE SEA LEVEL

Over 500 m
300 - 500 m
200 - 300 m
100 - 200 m
0 - 100 m

DEPTHS BELOW LAKE LEVEL

0 - 100 m
100 - 200 m
Over 200 m

Metres	Feet
100	328
200	656
300	984
500	1640

SCALE 1:5 000 000

0 50 100 150 200 250 kilometres

0 25 50 75 100 125 150 175 miles

The Great Lakes – Superior, Michigan, Huron, Erie and Ontario – are an important part of the physical and cultural heritage of North America. Spanning more than 1,200 kilometres (750 miles) from west to east, these vast inland freshwater seas have provided water for consumption, transportation, power, recreation and a host of other uses.

The water of the lakes and the many resources of the Great Lakes basin have played a major role in the history and development of the United States and Canada. For the early European explorers and settlers, the lakes and their tributaries were the avenues for penetrating the continent, extracting valued resources and carrying local products abroad.

Now the Great Lakes basin is home to more than one-tenth of the population of the United States and one-quarter of the population of Canada. Some of the world's largest concentrations of industrial capacity are located in the Great Lakes region. Nearly 25 percent of the total Canadian agricultural production and 7 percent of the American production are located in the basin. The United States considers the Great Lakes a fourth seacoast, and the Great Lakes region is a dominant factor in the Canadian industrial economy.

PHYSICAL CHARACTERISTICS OF THE SYSTEM

The magnitude of the Great Lakes water system is difficult to appreciate, even for those who live within the basin. The lakes contain about 23,000 km³ (5,500 cu. mi.) of water, covering a total area of 244,000 km² (94,000 sq. mi.) The Great Lakes are the largest system of fresh, surface water on earth, containing roughly 18 percent of the world supply. Only the polar ice caps contain more fresh water.

In spite of their large size, the Great Lakes are sensitive to the effects of a wide range of pollutants. The sources of pollution include the runoff of soils and farm chemicals from agricultural lands, the waste from cities, discharges from industrial areas and leachate from disposal sites. The large surface area of the lakes also makes them vulnerable to direct atmospheric pollutants that fall with rain or snow and as dust on the lake surface.

INTRODUCTION: *the* GREAT LAKES

The northern region of the Great Lakes is sparsely populated and is characterized by coniferous forest and rocky shorelines. Above, the western shore of Georgian Bay in the Bruce Peninsula National Park.

Outflows from the Great Lakes are relatively small (less than 1 percent per year) in comparison with the total volume of water. Pollutants that enter the lakes – whether by direct discharge along the shores, through tributaries, from land use or from the atmosphere – are retained in the system and become more concentrated with time. Also, pollutants remain in the system because of resuspension (or mixing back into the water) of sediment and cycling through biological food chains.

Because of the large size of the watershed, physical characteristics such as climate, soils and topography vary across the basin. To the north, the climate is cold and the terrain is dominated by a granite bedrock called the Canadian (or Laurentian) Shield consisting of Precambrian rocks under a generally thin layer of acidic soils. Conifers dominate the northern forests.

In the southern areas of the basin, the climate is much warmer. The soils are deeper with layers or mixtures of clays, silts, sands, gravels and boulders deposited as glacial drift or as glacial lake and river sediments. The lands are usually fertile and can be readily drained for agriculture. The original deciduous forests have given way to agriculture and sprawling urban development.

Although part of a single system, each lake is different. In volume, Lake Superior is the largest. It is also the deepest and coldest of the five. Superior could contain all the other Great Lakes and three more Lake Eries. Because of its size, Superior has a retention time of 191 years. Retention time is a measure based on the volume of water in the lake and the mean rate of outflow. Most of the Superior basin is forested, with little agriculture because of a cool climate and poor soils. The forests and sparse population result in relatively few pollutants entering Lake Superior, except through airborne transport.

Lake Michigan, the second largest, is the only Great Lake entirely within the United States. The northern part is in the colder, less developed upper Great Lakes region. It is sparsely populated, except for the Fox River Valley, which drains into Green Bay. This bay has one of the most productive Great Lakes fisheries but receives the wastes from the world's largest concentration of pulp and paper mills. The more temperate southern basin of Lake Michigan is among the most urbanized areas in the Great Lakes system. It contains the Milwaukee and Chicago metropolitan areas. This region is home to about 8 million people or about one-fifth of the total population of the Great Lakes basin.

Lake Huron, which includes Georgian Bay, is the third largest of the lakes by volume. Many Canadians and Americans own cottages on the shallow, sandy beaches of Huron and along the rocky shores of Georgian Bay. The Saginaw River basin is intensively farmed and contains the Flint and Saginaw-Bay City metropolitan areas. Saginaw Bay, like Green Bay, contains a very productive fishery.

Lake Erie is the smallest of the lakes in volume and is exposed to the greatest effects from urbanization and agriculture. Because of the fertile soils surrounding the lake, the area is intensively farmed. The lake receives runoff from the agricultural area of southwestern Ontario and parts of Ohio, Indiana and Michigan. Seventeen metropolitan areas with populations over 50,000 are located within the Lake Erie basin. Although the area of the lake is about 26,000 km² (10,000 square miles), the average depth is only about 19 metres (62 feet). It is the shallowest of the five lakes and therefore warms rapidly in the spring and summer, and frequently freezes over in winter. It also has the shortest retention time of the lakes, 2.6 years. The western basin, comprising about one-fifth of the lake, is very shallow with an average depth of 7.4 metres (24 feet) and a maximum depth of 19 metres (62 feet).

Lake Ontario, although slightly smaller in area, is much deeper than its upstream neighbor, Lake Erie, with an average depth of 86 metres (283 feet) and a retention time of about 6 years. Major urban industrial centers, such as Hamilton and Toronto, are located on its shore. The U.S. shore is less urbanized and is not intensively farmed, except for a narrow band along the lake.

SETTLEMENT

The modern history of the Great Lakes region, from discovery and settlement by European immigrants to the present day, can be viewed not only as a progression of intensifying use of a vast natural resource, but also as a process of learning about the Great Lakes ecosystem. At first it was a matter of making use of the natural resources of the basin while avoiding its dangers. Not until much later, when the watershed was more intensively settled and exploited, was it learned that abuse of the waters and the basin could result in great damage to the entire system.

EXPLOITATION

The first Europeans found a relatively stable ecosystem, which had evolved during the 10,000 years since the retreat of the last glacier; a system that was only moderately disturbed by the hunting and agricultural activities of the native peoples. The first European arrivals had a modest impact on the system, limited to the exploitation of some fur-bearing animals. However, the following waves of immigrants logged, farmed and fished commercially in the region, bringing about profound ecological changes. The mature forests were clear-cut from the watersheds, soil was laid bare by the plow, and the undisturbed fish populations were harvested indiscriminately by an awesome new predator – humans with nets.

As settlement and exploitation intensified, portions of the system were drastically changed. Logging removed

protective shade from streams and left them blocked with debris. Sawmills left streams and embayments clogged with sawdust. When the land was plowed for farming the exposed soils washed away more readily,

burying valuable stream and river mouth habitats. Exploitive fishing began to reduce the seemingly endless abundance of fish stocks, and whole populations of fish began to disappear.

Great Lakes Factsheet No. 1
Physical Features And Population

		Superior	Michigan	Huron	Erie	Ontario	Totals
Elevation[a]	(feet)**	600	577	577	569	243	
	(metres)	183	176	176	173	74	
Length	(miles)*	350	307	206	241	193	
	(kilometres)	563	494	332	388	311	
Breadth	(miles)*	160	118	183	57	53	
	(kilometres)	257	190	245	92	85	
Average Depth[a]	(feet)**	483	279	195	62	283	
	(metres)	147	85	59	19	86	
Maximum Depth[a]	(feet)*	1,332	925	750	210	802	
	(metres)	406	282	229	64	244	
Volume[a]	(cu. miles)*	2,900	1,180	850	116	393	5,439
	(km³)	12,100	4,920	3,540	484	1,640	22,684
AREA							
Water	(sq. mi.)*	31,700	22,300	23,000	9,910	7,340	94,250
	(km²)	82,100	57,800	59,600	25,700	18,960	244,160
Land Drainage Area[b]	(sq. mi.)*	49,300	45,600	51,700	30,140	24,720	201,460
	(km²)	127,700	118,000	134,100	78,000	64,030	521,830
Total	(sq. mi.)*	81,000	67,900	74,700	40,050	32,060	295,710
	(km²)	209,800	175,800	193,700	103,700	82,990	765,990
Shoreline Length[c]	(miles)*	2,726	1,638	3,827	871	712	10,210[d]
	(kilometres)	4,385	2,633	6,157	1,402	1,146	17,017[d]
Retention Time	(years)**	191	99	22	2.6	6	
Population: U.S. (1990)[†]		425,548	10,057,026	1,502,687	10,017,530	2,704,284	24,707,075
Canada (1991)		181,573		1,191,467	1,664,639	5,446,611	8,484,290
Totals		607,121	10,057,026	2,694,154	11,682,169	8,150,895	33,191,365
Outlet		St. Marys River	Straits of Mackinac	St. Clair River	Niagara River Welland Canal	St. Lawrence River	

Notes:

[a] Measured at Low Water Datum.

[b] Land Drainage Area for Lake Huron includes St. Marys River.

Lake Erie includes the St. Clair-Detroit system.

Lake Ontario includes the Niagara River.

[c] Including islands.

[d] These totals are greater than the sum of the shoreline length for the lakes because they include the connecting channels (excluding the St. Lawrence River).

Sources: * Coordinating Committee on Great Lakes Basic Hydraulic and Hydrologic Data, COORDINATED GREAT LAKES PHYSICAL DATA. May, 1992

** EXTENSION BULLETINS E-1866-70, Michigan Sea Grant College Program, Cooperative Extension Service, Michigan State University, E. Lansing, Michigan, 1985

[†] 1990-1991 population census data were collected on different watershed boundaries and are not directly comparable to previous years.

INDUSTRIALIZATION

Industrialization followed close behind agrarian settlement, and the virtually untreated wastes of early industrialization degraded one river after another. The growing urbanization that accompanied industrial development added to the degradation of water quality, creating nuisance conditions such as bacterial contamination, putrescence and floating debris in rivers and nearshore areas. In some situations, the resulting contaminated drinking water and polluted beaches contributed to fatal human epidemics of waterborne diseases such as typhoid fever. Nonetheless, the problems were perceived as being local in nature.

As industrialization progressed and as agriculture intensified after the turn of the 20th century, new chemical substances came into use, such as PCBs (polychlorinated biphenyls) in the 1920s and DDT (dichloro-diphenyl-trichloroethane) in the 1940s. Non-organic fertilizers were used to enrich the already fertile soils to enhance production. The combination of synthetic fertilizers, existing sources of nutrient-rich organic pollutants, such as untreated human wastes from cities, and phosphate detergents caused an acceleration of biological production (eutrophication) in the lakes. In the 1950s, Lake Erie showed the first evidence of lake-wide eutrophic imbalance with massive algal blooms and the depletion of oxygen.

THE EVOLUTION OF GREAT LAKES MANAGEMENT

In the late 1960s, growing public concern about the deterioration of water quality in the Great Lakes stimulated new investment in pollution research, especially the problems of eutrophication and DDT. Governments responded to the concern by controlling and regulating pollutant discharges and assisting with the construction of municipal sewage treatment works. This concern was formalized in the first Great Lakes Water Quality Agreement between Canada and the U.S. in 1972.

Major reductions were made in pollutant discharges in the 1970s. The results were visible. Nuisance conditions occurred

Industrialization of the Great Lakes basin followed early settlement and the growth in agriculture. Above, a river winds its way through an industrial city in the basin (ca. 1970).

less frequently as floating debris and oil slicks began to disappear. Dissolved oxygen levels improved, eliminating odor problems. Many beaches reopened as a result of improved sewage control, and algal mats disappeared as nutrient levels declined. The initiatives of the 1970s showed that improvements could be made and provided several important lessons beyond the cleanup of localized nuisance conditions.

First, the problem of algal growth in the lakes caused by accelerated eutrophication required a lake-wide approach to measure the amount of the critical nutrient, phosphorus, entering and leaving each lake from all sources and outlets. This approach of calculating a 'mass balance' of the substance was then combined with other research and mathematical modeling to set target loading limits for phosphorus entering the lake (or portions of the lake). The target load is the amount of phosphorus that will

not cause excessive algal growth (i.e., an amount that could safely be assimilated by the ecosystem).

Other major lessons learned about the system resulted from research on toxic substances, initially the pesticide DDT. Toxic contaminants include persistent organic chemicals and metals. These substances enter the lakes directly from discharges of sewage and industrial effluents and indirectly from waste sites, diffuse land runoff and atmospheric deposition. As a result of increased research, sampling and surveillance, toxic substances have been found to be a system-wide problem.

TOXIC CONTAMINANTS

Toxic contaminants pose a threat not only to aquatic and wildlife species, but to human health as well, since humans are at the top of many food chains. Some toxic substances biologically accumulate or are magnified as they move through the food chain. Consequently, top predators such as lake trout and fish-eating birds – cormorants, ospreys and herring gulls – can receive extremely high exposures to these contaminants. Concentrations of toxic substances can be millions of times higher in these species than in water. As a result, the potential for human exposure to these contaminants is far greater from consumption of contaminated fish and wildlife than from drinking water.

Aquatic and wildlife species have been intensively studied, and adverse effects such as cross-bills and egg-shell thinning in birds, and tumors in fish are well documented. There is less certainty about the risk to human health of long-term exposure to low levels of toxic pollutants in the lakes, but there is no disagreement that the risk to human health will increase if toxic contaminants continue to accumulate in the Great Lakes ecosystem. Long-term, low-level exposures are of concern because of subtle effects that toxic contaminants may have on reproduction, the immune system and development in children. Relationships between environmental contaminants and diseases such as cancer are also of concern.

UNDERSTANDING THE LAKES FROM AN ECOSYSTEM PERSPECTIVE

The ecosystem approach, together with an increased emphasis on toxic substances, was given formal recognition in the second Great Lakes Water Quality Agreement, signed in 1978. In 1987, management aspects of the ecosystem approach were further defined in revisions to the Agreement, calling for management plans to restore fourteen beneficial uses. The beneficial uses to be restored include unimpaired use of the ecosystem by all living components, including humans.

The Agreement called for Remedial Action Plans (RAPs) to be prepared for geographic Areas of Concern (AOCs) where local use impairments exist. It also called for Lakewide Management Plans to be prepared for critical pollutants that affect whole lakes or large portions of them. The purpose of these management plans is to clearly identify the key steps needed to restore and protect the lakes.

To measure restoration of ecosystem recovery, the 1987 Agreement revisions added a call for ecosystem objectives and indicators to complement the chemical objectives already provided in the Agreement. These biological measures of ecosystem integrity provide an important element of the ecosystem approach and are being developed as part of the process for developing lake-wide management plans. Ecosystem indicators have already been

adopted for Lake Superior. These indicators are organisms (such as bird or fish populations) that tell us whether the ecosystem is healthy and whether these populations are stable and self-reproducing.

The concepts of mass balance, system-wide contamination and bioaccumulation in the food chain have become essential components in understanding the lakes from an ecosystem perspective. For example, the mass balance approach to phosphorus control has been used to formulate target pollutant loadings for the lower lakes.

Over 33 million people who live in the Great Lakes basin and their governments face an immense challenge for the future of the basin. The wise management needed to maintain the use of Great Lakes resources requires greater public awareness, the forging of political will to protect the lakes, and creative government action and cooperation. It will not be easy.

The Great Lakes are surrounded by two sovereign nations, a Canadian province, eight American states and thousands of local, regional and special-purpose governing bodies with jurisdiction for management of some aspect of the basin or the lakes. Cooperation is essential because problems such as water consumption, diversions, lake levels and shoreline management do not respect political boundaries.

With this in mind, public consultations that include residents, private organizations, industry and government are considered to be an essential part of the decision-making process for managing the resources of the Great Lakes ecosystem. Residents of the basin have been empowered to participate in the problem-solving process, promote healthy sustainable environments and reduce their personal exposure to Great Lakes contaminants.

Humans are part of and depend on the natural ecosystem of the Great Lakes, but may be damaging the capacity of the system to renew and sustain itself and the life within it. Protection of the lakes for future use requires a greater understanding of how past problems developed, as well as continued remedial action to prevent further damage.

GEOLOGY AND MINERAL RESOURCES

STAGES IN THE EVOLUTION OF THE GREAT LAKES

SCALE 1: 20 000 000

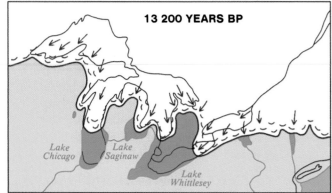

13 200 YEARS BP

Lake Chicago, Lake Saginaw, Lake Whittlesey

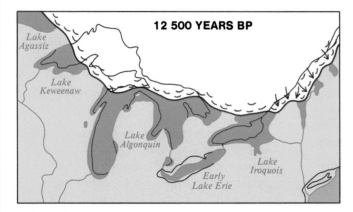

12 500 YEARS BP

Lake Agassiz, Lake Keweenaw, Lake Algonquin, Early Lake Erie, Lake Iroquois

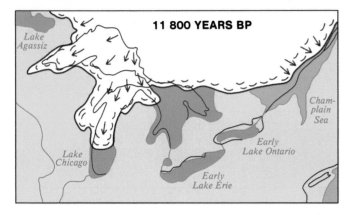

11 800 YEARS BP

Lake Agassiz, Lake Chicago, Early Lake Erie, Early Lake Ontario, Champlain Sea

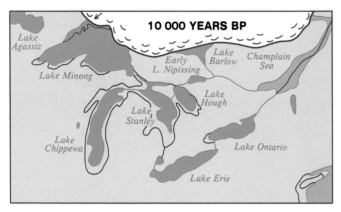

10 000 YEARS BP

Lake Agassiz, Lake Minong, Early L. Nipissing, Lake Barlow, Lake Stanley, Lake Hough, Champlain Sea, Lake Chippewa, Lake Ontario, Lake Erie

NOTE:
The maps on left are "snapshots" of a continuously changing situation during the retreat of the Wisconsin icesheet. They should not be viewed as a simple sequence, since many intermediate stages are omitted. The letters BP denote before present.

Legend:
- Ice
- Ice Front
- Advancing Ice
- Fresh Water
- Salt Water
- Present Coastline

GLACIAL DEPOSITS

SCALE 1: 20 000 000

Stratified Drift
- Silt and Clay (glacial lake deposits)
- Sand and Gravel (outwash, alluvial and ice contact deposits)

Unstratified Drift
- Till (ground and end moraines)

Bedrock areas where the glacial cover is absent (e.g. parts of Canadian Shield) are not distinguished.

SCALE 1: 7 500 000

0   100   200   300 kilometres
0   50   100   150   200 miles

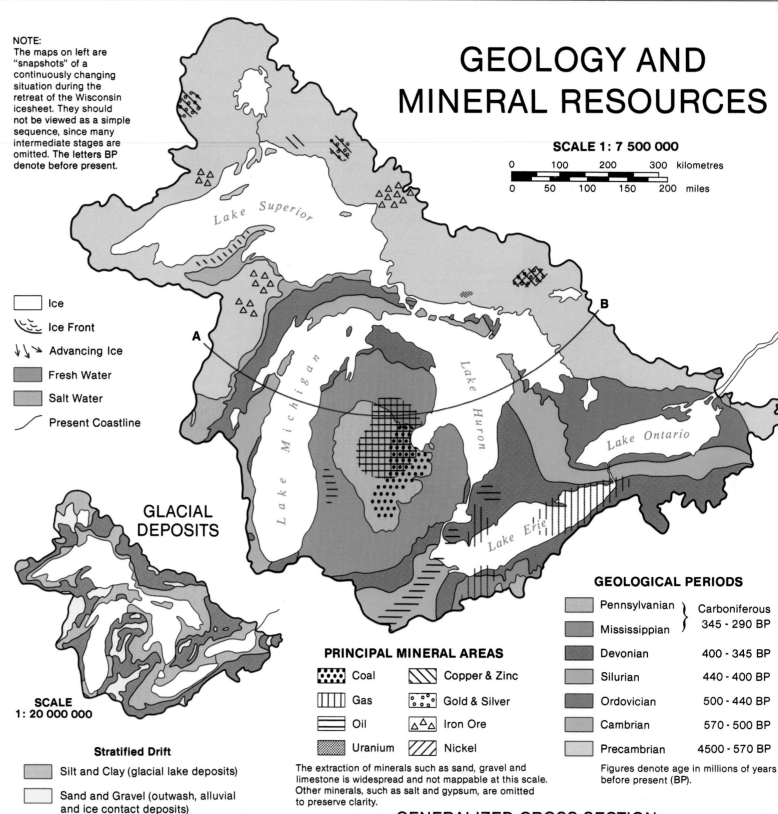

Lake Superior, Lake Michigan, Lake Huron, Lake Ontario, Lake Erie

PRINCIPAL MINERAL AREAS
- Coal
- Gas
- Oil
- Uranium
- Copper & Zinc
- Gold & Silver
- Iron Ore
- Nickel

The extraction of minerals such as sand, gravel and limestone is widespread and not mappable at this scale. Other minerals, such as salt and gypsum, are omitted to preserve clarity.

GEOLOGICAL PERIODS

Period	Age
Pennsylvanian	Carboniferous 345 - 290 BP
Mississippian	
Devonian	400 - 345 BP
Silurian	440 - 400 BP
Ordovician	500 - 440 BP
Cambrian	570 - 500 BP
Precambrian	4500 - 570 BP

Figures denote age in millions of years before present (BP).

GENERALIZED CROSS-SECTION

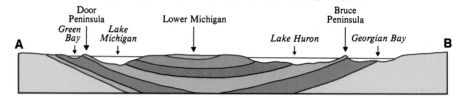

A — Green Bay, Door Peninsula, Lake Michigan, Lower Michigan, Lake Huron, Bruce Peninsula, Georgian Bay — B

Brock University Cartograph

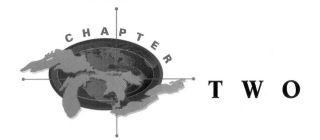
GEOLOGY

The foundation for the present Great Lakes basin was set about 3 billion years ago, during the Precambrian Era. This era occupies about five-sixths of all geological time and was a period of great volcanic activity and tremendous stresses, which formed great mountain systems. Early sedimentary and volcanic rocks were folded and heated into complex structures. These were later eroded and, today, appear as the gently rolling hills and small mountain remnants of the Canadian Shield, which forms the northern and northwestern portions of the Great Lakes basin. Granitic rocks of the shield extend southward beneath the Paleozoic, sedimentary rocks where they form the 'basement' structure of the southern and eastern portions of the basin.

With the coming of the Paleozoic Era, most of central North America was flooded

Layers of sedimentary rock eroded by wind and wave action are revealed in these formations at Flower Pot Island at the tip of the Bruce Peninsula in Canada.

NATURAL PROCESSES
in the
GREAT LAKES

again and again by marine seas, which were inhabited by a multitude of life forms, including corals, crinoids, brachiopods and mollusks. The seas deposited lime silts, clays, sand and salts, which eventually consolidated into limestone, shales, sandstone, halite and gypsum.

During the Pleistocene Epoch, the continental glaciers repeatedly advanced over the Great Lakes region from the north. The first glacier began to advance more than a million years ago. As they inched forward, the glaciers, up to 2,000 metres (6,500 feet) thick, scoured the surface of the earth, leveled hills, and altered forever the previous ecosystem. Valleys created by the river systems of the previous era were deepened and enlarged to form the basins for the Great Lakes. Thousands of years later, the climate began to warm, melting and slowly shrinking the glacier. This was followed by an interglacial period during which vegetation and wildlife returned. The whole cycle was repeated several times.

Sand, silt, clay and boulders deposited by the glaciers occur in various mixtures and forms. These deposits are collectively referred to as 'glacial drift' and include features such as moraines, which are linear mounds of poorly sorted material or 'till', flat till plains, till drumlins, and eskers formed of well-sorted sands and gravels deposited from meltwater. Areas having substantial deposits of well-sorted sands and gravels (eskers,

kames and outwash) are usually significant groundwater storage and transmission areas called 'aquifers'. These also serve as excellent sources of sand and gravel for commercial extraction.

As the glacier retreated, large volumes of meltwater occurred along the front of the ice. Because the land was greatly depressed at this time from the weight of the glacier, large glacial lakes formed. These lakes were much larger than the present Great Lakes. Their legacy can still be seen in the form of beach ridges, eroded bluffs and flat plains located hundreds of metres above present lake levels. Glacial lake plains known as 'lacustrine plains' occur around Saginaw Bay and west and north of Lake Erie.

As the glacier receded, the land began to rise. This uplift (at times relatively rapid) and the shifting ice fronts caused dramatic changes in the depth, size and drainage patterns of the glacial lakes. Drainage from the lakes occurred variously through the Illinois River Valley (towards the Mississippi River), the Hudson River Valley, the Kawartha Lakes (Trent River) and the Ottawa River Valley before entering their present outlet through the St. Lawrence River Valley. Although the uplift has slowed considerably, it is still occurring in the northern portion of the basin. This, along with changing long-term weather patterns, suggests that the lakes are not static and will continue to evolve.

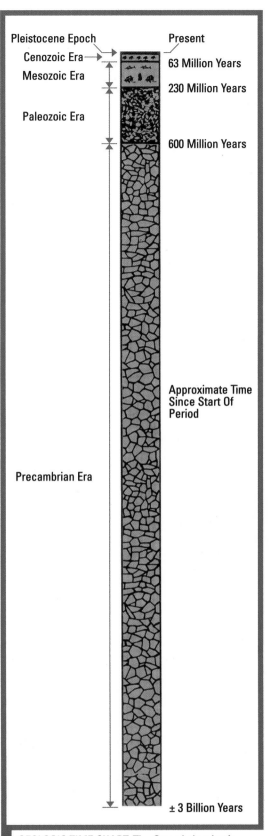

Pleistocene Epoch	Present
Cenozoic Era	63 Million Years
Mesozoic Era	230 Million Years
Paleozoic Era	600 Million Years
	Approximate Time Since Start Of Period
Precambrian Era	
	± 3 Billion Years

GEOLOGIC TIME CHART. The Great Lakes basin is a relatively young ecosystem having formed during the last 10,000 years. Its foundation was laid through many millions of years and several geologic eras. This chart gives a relative idea of the age of the eras.

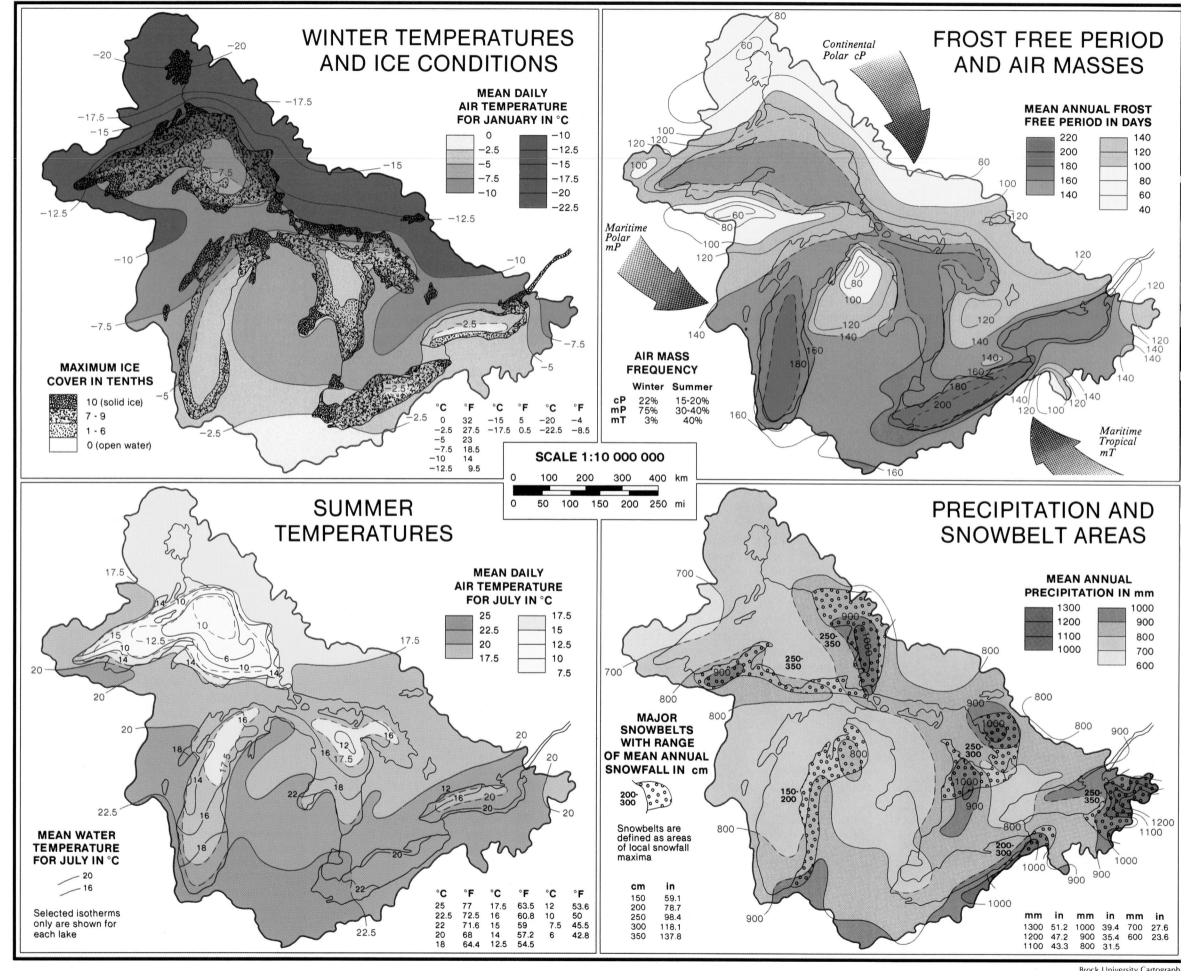

WINTER TEMPERATURES AND ICE CONDITIONS

MEAN DAILY AIR TEMPERATURE FOR JANUARY IN °C

0	-10
-2.5	-12.5
-5	-15
-7.5	-17.5
-10	-20
	-22.5

MAXIMUM ICE COVER IN TENTHS

- 10 (solid ice)
- 7 - 9
- 1 - 6
- 0 (open water)

°C	°F	°C	°F	°C	°F
0	32	-15	5	-20	-4
-2.5	27.5	-17.5	0.5	-22.5	-8.5
-5	23				
-7.5	18.5				
-10	14				
-12.5	9.5				

FROST FREE PERIOD AND AIR MASSES

Continental Polar cP

Maritime Polar mP

Maritime Tropical mT

MEAN ANNUAL FROST FREE PERIOD IN DAYS

220	140
200	120
180	100
160	80
140	60
	40

AIR MASS FREQUENCY

	Winter	Summer
cP	22%	15-20%
mP	75%	30-40%
mT	3%	40%

SCALE 1:10 000 000

0 100 200 300 400 km

0 50 100 150 200 250 mi

SUMMER TEMPERATURES

MEAN DAILY AIR TEMPERATURE FOR JULY IN °C

25	17.5
22.5	15
20	12.5
17.5	10
	7.5

MEAN WATER TEMPERATURE FOR JULY IN °C

— 20
— 16

Selected isotherms only are shown for each lake

°C	°F	°C	°F	°C	°F
25	77	17.5	63.5	12	53.6
22.5	72.5	16	60.8	10	50
22	71.6	15	59	7.5	45.5
20	68	14	57.2	6	42.8
18	64.4	12.5	54.5		

PRECIPITATION AND SNOWBELT AREAS

MEAN ANNUAL PRECIPITATION IN mm

1300	1000
1200	900
1100	800
1000	700
	600

MAJOR SNOWBELTS WITH RANGE OF MEAN ANNUAL SNOWFALL IN cm

200-300

Snowbelts are defined as areas of local snowfall maxima

cm	in
150	59.1
200	78.7
250	98.4
300	118.1
350	137.8

mm	in	mm	in	mm	in
1300	51.2	1000	39.4	700	27.6
1200	47.2	900	35.4	600	23.6
1100	43.3	800	31.5		

Brock University Cartograph

CLIMATE

The weather in the Great Lakes basin is affected by three factors: air masses from other regions, the location of the basin within a large continental landmass, and the moderating influence of the lakes themselves. The prevailing movement of air is from the west. The characteristically changeable weather of the region is the result of alternating flows of warm, humid air from the Gulf of Mexico and cold, dry air from the Arctic.

In summer, the northern region around Lake Superior generally receives cool, dry air masses from the Canadian northwest. In the south, tropical air masses originating in the Gulf of Mexico are most influential. As the Gulf air crosses the lakes, the bottom layers remain cool while the top layers are warmed. Occasionally, the upper layer traps the cooler air below, which in turn traps moisture and airborne pollutants, and prevents them from rising and dispersing. This is called a temperature inversion and can result in dank, humid days in areas in the midst of the basin, such as Michigan and Southern Ontario, and can also cause smog in low-lying industrial areas.

Winter on the lakes is characterized by alternating flows of frigid arctic air and moderating air masses from the Gulf of Mexico. Heavy snowfalls frequently occur on the lee side of the lakes.

Increased summer sunshine warms the surface layer of water in the lakes, making it lighter than the colder water below. In the fall and winter months, release of the heat stored in the lakes moderates the climate near the shores of the lakes. Parts of Southern Ontario, Michigan and western New York enjoy milder winters than similar mid-continental areas at lower latitudes.

In the autumn, the rapid movement and occasional clash of warm and cold air masses through the region produce strong winds. Air temperatures begin to drop gradually and less sunlight, combined with increased cloudiness, signal more storms and precipitation. Late autumn storms are often the most perilous for navigation and shipping on the lakes.

In winter, the Great Lakes region is affected by two major air masses. Arctic air from the northwest is very cold and dry when it enters the basin, but is warmed and picks up moisture traveling over the comparatively warmer lakes. When it reaches the land, the moisture condenses as snow, creating heavy snowfalls on the lee side of the lakes in areas frequently referred to as snowbelts. For part of the winter, the region is affected by Pacific air masses that have lost much of their moisture crossing the western mountains. Less frequently, air masses enter the basin from the southwest, bringing in moisture from the Gulf of Mexico. This air is slightly warmer and more humid. During the winter, the temperature of the lakes continues to drop. Ice frequently covers Lake Erie but seldom fully covers the other lakes.

Spring in the Great Lakes region, like autumn, is characterized by variable weather. Alternating air masses move through rapidly, resulting in frequent cloud cover and thunderstorms. By early spring, the warmer air and increased sunshine begin to melt the snow and lake ice, starting again the thermal layering of the lakes. The lakes are slower to warm than the land and tend to keep adjacent land areas cool, thus prolonging cool conditions sometimes well into April. Most years, this delays the leafing and blossoming of plants, protecting tender plants, such as fruit trees, from late frosts. This extended state of dormancy allows plants from somewhat warmer climates to survive in the western shadow of the lakes. It is also the reason for the presence of vineyards in those areas.

CLIMATE CHANGE AND THE GREAT LAKES

At various times throughout its history, the Great Lakes basin has been covered by thick glaciers and tropical forests, but these changes occurred before humans occupied the basin. Present-day concern about the atmosphere is premised on the belief that society at large, through its means of production and modes of daily activity, especially by ever increasing carbon dioxide emissions, may be modifying the climate at a rate unprecedented in history.

The very prevalent 'greenhouse effect' is actually a natural phenomenon. It is a process by which water vapor and carbon dioxide in the atmosphere absorb heat given off by the earth and radiate it back to the surface. Consequently the earth remains warm and habitable (16°C average world temperature rather than −18°C without the greenhouse effect). However, humans have increased the carbon dioxide present in the atmosphere since the industrial revolution from 280 parts per million to the present 350 ppm, and some predict that the concentration will reach twice its pre-industrial levels by the middle of the next century.

Climatologists, using the General Circulation Model (GCM), have been able to determine the manner in which the increase of carbon dioxide emissions will affect the climate in the Great Lakes basin. Several of these models exist and show that at twice the carbon dioxide level, the climate of the basin will be warmer by 2–4°C and slightly damper than at present. For example, Toronto's climate would resemble the present climate of southern Ohio. Warmer climates mean increased evaporation from the lake surfaces and evapotranspiration from the land surface of the basin. This in turn will augment the percentage of precipitation that is returned to the atmosphere. Studies have shown that the resulting net basin supply, the amount of water contributed by each lake basin to the overall hydrologic system, will be decreased by 23 to 50 percent. The resulting decreases in average lake levels will be from half a metre to two metres, depending on the GCM used.

Large declines in lake levels would create large-scale economic concern for the commercial users of the water system. Shipping companies and hydroelectric power companies would suffer economic repercus-sions, and harbors and marinas would be adversely affected. While the precision of such projections remains uncertain, the possibility of their accuracy embraces important long-term implications for the Great Lakes.

The potential effects of climate change on human health in the Great Lakes region are also of concern, and researchers can only speculate as to what might occur. For example, weather disturbances, drought, and changes in temperature and growing season could affect crops and food production in the basin. Changes in air pollution patterns as a result of climate change could affect respiratory health, causing asthma, and new disease vectors and agents could migrate into the region.

THE HYDROLOGIC CYCLE

Water is a renewable resource. It is continually replenished in ecosystems through the hydrologic cycle. Water evaporates in contact with dry air, forming water vapor. The vapor can remain as a gas, contributing to the humidity of the atmosphere; or it can condense and form water droplets, which, if they remain in the air, form fog and clouds. In the Great Lakes basin, much of the moisture in the region evaporates from the surface of the lakes. Other sources of moisture include the surface of small lakes and tributaries, moisture on the land mass and water released by plants. Global movements of air also carry moisture into the basin, especially from the tropics.

Moisture-bearing air masses move through the basin and deposit their moisture as rain, snow, hail or sleet. Some of this precipitation returns to the atmosphere and some falls on the surfaces of the Great Lakes to become part of the vast quantity of stored fresh water once again. Precipitation that falls on the land returns to the lakes as surface runoff or infiltrates the soil and becomes groundwater.

Whether it becomes surface runoff or groundwater depends upon a number of factors. Sandy soils, gravels and some rock types contribute to groundwater flows, whereas clays and impermeable rocks contribute to surface runoff. Water falling on sloped areas tends to run off rapidly, while water falling on flat areas tends to

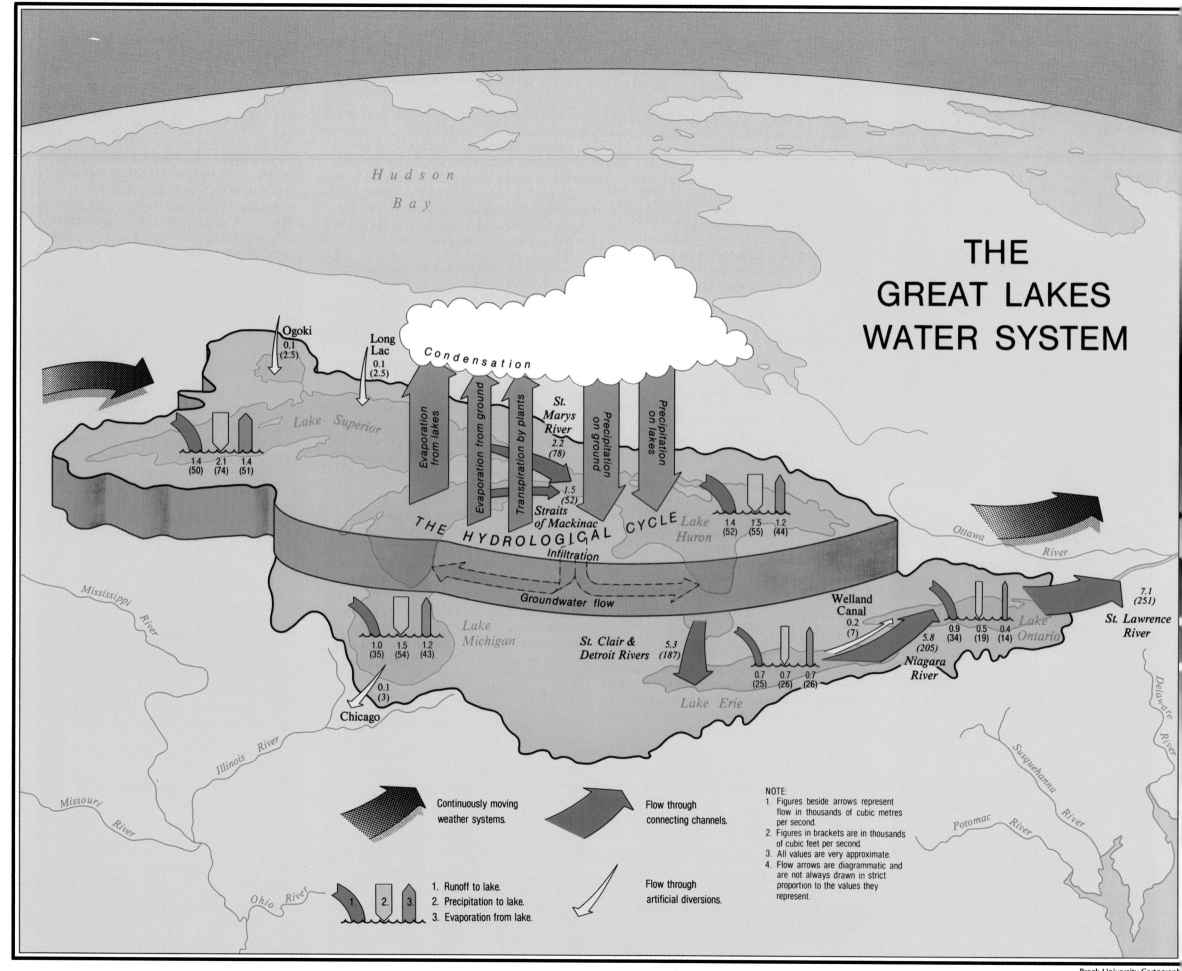

THE GREAT LAKES WATER SYSTEM

Hudson Bay

Condensation

THE HYDROLOGICAL CYCLE

Ogoki
0.1
(2.5)

Long Lac
0.1
(2.5)

Lake Superior

Evaporation from lakes

Evaporation from ground

Transpiration by plants

St. Marys River
2.2
(78)

Precipitation on ground

Precipitation on lakes

Straits of Mackinac
1.5
(52)

Lake Huron

1.4
(50) 2.1
(74) 1.4
(51)

1.4
(52) 1.5
(55) 1.2
(44)

Infiltration

Groundwater flow

Ottawa River

Welland Canal
0.2
(7)

7.1
(251)

St. Lawrence River

Lake Michigan

1.0
(35) 1.5
(54) 1.2
(43)

St. Clair & Detroit Rivers
5.3
(187)

Niagara River
5.8
(205)

Lake Ontario
0.9
(34) 0.5
(19) 0.4
(14)

Mississippi River

0.7
(25) 0.7
(26) 0.7
(26)

Lake Erie

0.1
(3)

Chicago

Illinois River

Missouri River

Ohio River

Delaware River

Susquehanna River

Potomac River

Continuously moving weather systems.

Flow through connecting channels.

1. Runoff to lake.
2. Precipitation to lake.
3. Evaporation from lake.

Flow through artificial diversions.

NOTE:
1. Figures beside arrows represent flow in thousands of cubic metres per second.
2. Figures in brackets are in thousands of cubic feet per second.
3. All values are very approximate.
4. Flow arrows are diagrammatic and are not always drawn in strict proportion to the values they represent.

Thousands of tributaries feed the Great Lakes, replenishing the vast supply of stored fresh water.

be absorbed or stored on the surface. Vegetation also tends to decrease surface runoff; root systems hold moisture-laden soil readily, and water remains on plants.

SURFACE RUNOFF

Surface runoff is a major factor in the character of the Great Lakes basin. Rain falling on exposed soil tilled for agriculture or cleared for construction accelerates erosion and the transport of soil particles and pollutants into tributaries. Suspended soil particles in water are deposited as sediment in the lakes and often collect near the mouths of tributaries and connecting channels. Much of the sediment deposited in nearshore areas is resuspended and carried farther into the lake during storms. The finest particles (clays and silts) may remain in suspension long enough to reach the mid-lake areas.

Before settlement of the basin, streams typically ran clear year-round because natural vegetation prevented soil loss. Clearing of the original forest for agriculture and logging has resulted in both more erosion and runoff into the streams and lakes. This accelerated runoff aggravates flooding problems.

Wetlands

Wetlands are areas where the water table occurs above or near the land surface for at least part of the year. When open water is present, it must be less than two metres deep (seven feet), and stagnant or slow moving. The presence of excessive amounts of water in wetland regions has given rise to hydric soils, as well as encouraged the predominance of water tolerant (hydrophytic) plants and similar biological activity.

Four basic types of wetland are encountered in the Great Lakes basin: swamps, marshes, bogs and fens. Swamps are areas where trees and shrubs live on wet, organically rich mineral soils that are flooded for part or all of the year. Marshes develop in shallow standing water such as ponds and protected bays. Aquatic plants (such as species of rushes) form thick stands, which are rooted in sediments or become floating mats where the water is deeper. Swamps and marshes occur most frequently in the southern and eastern portions of the basin.

Bogs form in shallow stagnant water. The most characteristic plant species are the sphagnum mosses, which tolerate conditions that are too acidic for most other organisms. Dead sphagnum decomposes very slowly, accumulating in mats that may eventually become many metres thick and form a dome well above the original surface of the water. It is this material that is excavated and sold as peat moss. Peat also accumulates in fens. Fens develop in shallow, slowly moving water. They are less acidic than bogs and are usually fed by groundwater. Fens are dominated by sedges and grasses, but may include shrubs and stunted trees. Fens and bogs are commonly referred to as 'peatlands' and occur most frequently in the cooler northern and northwestern portions of the Great Lakes basin.

Wetlands serve important roles ecologically, economically and socially to the overall health and maintenance of the Great Lakes ecosystem. They provide habitats for many kinds of plants and animals, some of which are found nowhere else. For ducks, geese and other migratory birds, wetlands are the most important part of the migratory cycle, providing food, resting places and seasonal habitats. Economically, wetlands play an essential role in sustaining a productive fishery. At least 32 of the 36 species of Great Lakes fish studied depend on coastal wetlands for their successful reproduction. In addition to providing a desirable habitat for aquatic life, wetlands prevent damage from erosion and flooding, as well as controlling point and nonpoint source pollution.

Coastal wetlands along the Great Lakes include some sites that are recognized internationally for their outstanding biological significance. Examples included the Long Point complex and Point Pelee on the north shore of Lake Erie and the National Wildlife Area on Lake St. Clair. Long Point also was designated a UNESCO Biosphere Reserve. Wetlands of the lower Great Lakes region have also been identified as a priority of the Eastern Habitat Joint Venture of the North American Waterfowl Management Plan, an international agreement between governments and non-government organizations (NGOs) to conserve highly significant wetlands.

Although wetlands are a fundamentally important element of the Great Lakes ecosystem and are of obvious merit, their numbers continue to decline at an alarming rate. Over two-thirds of the Great Lakes wetlands have already been lost and many of those remaining are threatened by development, drainage or pollution.

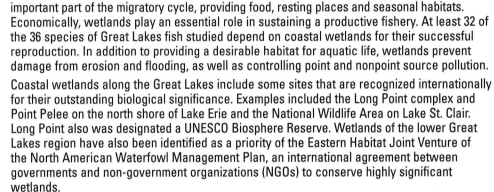

Long Point Marshes, Lake Erie.

GROUNDWATER

Groundwater is important to the Great Lakes ecosystem because it provides a reservoir for storing water and slowly replenishing the lakes in the form of base flow in the tributaries. It is also a source of drinking water for many communities in the Great Lakes basin. Shallow groundwater also provides moisture to plants.

As water passes through subsurface areas, some substances are filtered out, but some materials in the soils become dissolved or suspended in the water. Salts and minerals in the soil and bedrock are the source of what is referred to as 'hard' water, a common feature of well water in the lower Great Lakes basin.

Groundwater can also pick up materials of human origin that have been buried in dumps and landfill sites. Groundwater contamination problems can occur in both urban-industrial and agricultural areas. Protection and inspection of groundwater is essential to protect the quality of the entire water supply consumed by basin populations, because the underground movement of water is believed to be a major pathway for the transport of pollution to the Great Lakes. Groundwater may discharge directly to the lakes or indirectly as base flow to the tributaries.

LAKE LEVELS

The Great Lakes are part of the global hydrologic system. Prevailing westerly winds continuously carry moisture into the basin in air masses from other parts of the continent. At the same time, the basin loses moisture in departing air masses by evaporation and transpiration, and through the outflow of the St. Lawrence River. Over time, the quantity lost equals what is gained, but lake levels can vary substantially over short-term, seasonal and long-term periods.

Day-to-day changes are caused by winds that push water on shore. This is called 'wind set-up' and is usually associated with a major lake storm, which may last for hours or days. Another extreme form of oscillation, known as a 'seiche', occurs with rapid changes in winds and barometric pressure.

Annual or seasonal variations in water levels are based mainly on changes in precipitation and runoff to the Great Lakes. Generally, the lowest levels occur in winter when much of the precipitation is locked up in ice and snow on land, and dry winter air masses pass over the lakes enhancing evaporation. Levels are highest in summer after the spring thaw when runoff increases.

The irregular long-term cycles correspond to long-term trends in precipitation and temperature, the causes of which have yet to be adequately explained. Highest levels occur during periods of abundant precipitation and lower temperatures that decrease evaporation. During periods of high lake levels, storms cause considerable flooding and shoreline erosion, which often result in property damage. Much of the

During storms, high winds and rapid changes in barometric pressure cause severe wave conditions at shorelines.

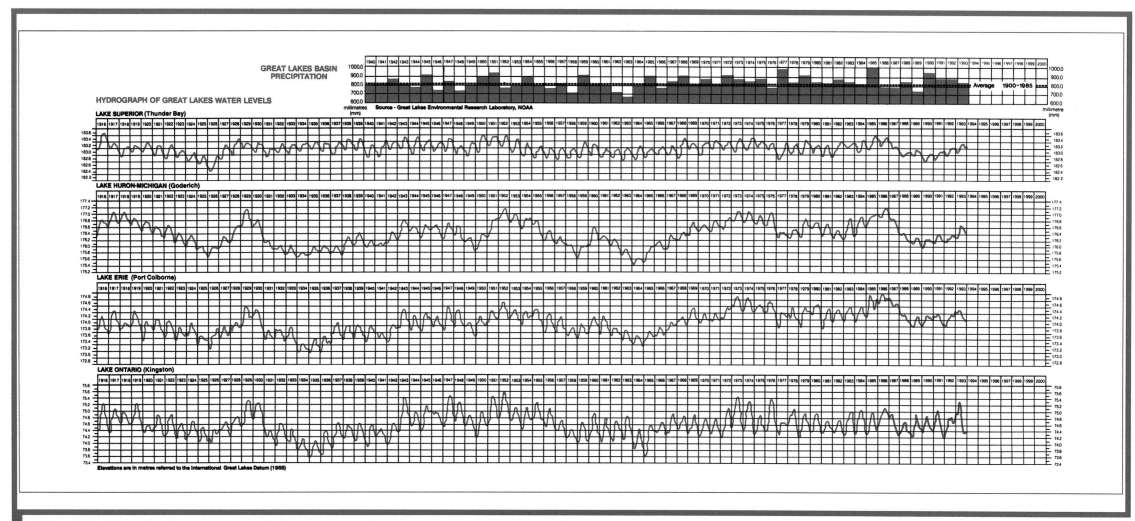

GREAT LAKES HYDROGRAPH. The Hydrograph for the Great Lakes shows the variations in water levels and the relationship of precipitation to water levels.

damage is attributable to intensive shore development, which alters protective dunes and wetlands, removes stabilizing vegetation, and generally reduces the ability of the shoreline to withstand the damaging effects of wind and waves.

The International Joint Commission, the binational agency established under the Boundary Waters Treaty of 1909 between Canada and the U.S., has the responsibility for regulation of flows on the St. Marys and the St. Lawrence Rivers. These channels have been altered by enlargement and placement of control works associated

High lake levels and severe weather conditions can cause damage to unprotected properties. Above, shoreline damage to the southern shore of Lake Michigan.

with deep-draft shipping. Agreements between the U.S. and Canada govern the flow through the control works on these connecting channels.

The water from Lake Michigan flows to Lake Huron through the Straits of Mackinac. These straits are deep and wide, resulting in Lakes Michigan and Huron standing at the same elevation. There are no artificial controls on the St. Clair and Detroit Rivers that could change the flow from the Michigan-Huron Lakes system into Lake Erie. The outflow of Lake Erie via the Niagara River is also uncontrolled, except for some diversion of water through the Welland Canal. A large percentage of the Niagara River flow is diverted through hydroelectric power plants at Niagara Falls, but this diversion has no effect on lake levels.

Studies of possible further regulation of flows and lake levels have concluded that natural fluctuation is huge compared with the influence of existing control works. Further regulation by engineering systems could not be justified in light of the cost and other impacts. Just one inch (two and a half centimetres) of water on the surface of Lakes Michigan and Huron amounts to more than 36 billion cubic metres of water (about 1,260 billion cubic feet).

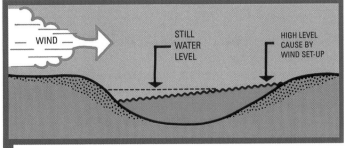

WIND SET-UP is a local rise in water caused by winds pushing water to one side of a lake.

LAKE PROCESSES: STRATIFICATION AND TURNOVER

The Great Lakes are not simply large containers of uniformly mixed water. They are, in fact, highly dynamic systems with complex processes and a variety of subsystems that change seasonally and on longer cycles.

The stratification or layering of water in the lakes is due to density changes caused by changes in temperature. The density of water increases as temperature decreases until it reaches its maximum density at about 4° Celsius (39° Fahrenheit). This causes thermal stratification, or the tendency of deep lakes to form distinct layers in the summer months. Deep water is insulated from the sun and stays cool and

more dense, forming a lower layer called the 'hypolimnion'. Surface and nearshore waters are warmed by the sun, making them less dense so that they form a surface layer called the 'epilimnion'. As the summer progresses, temperature differences increase between the layers. A thin middle layer, or 'thermocline', develops in which a rapid transition in temperature occurs.

The warm epilimnion supports most of the life in the lake. Algal production is greatest near the surface where the sun readily penetrates. The surface layer is also rich in oxygen, which is mixed into the water from the atmosphere. A second zone of high productivity exists just above the hypolimnion, due to upward diffusion of nutrients. The hypolimnion is less productive because it receives less sunlight. In some areas, such as the central basin of Lake Erie, it may lack oxygen because of decomposition of organic matter.

In late fall, surface waters cool, become denser and descend, displacing deep waters and causing a mixing or turnover of the entire lake. In winter, the temperature of the lower parts of the lake approaches 4° Celsius (39° Fahrenheit), while surface waters are cooled to the freezing point and ice can form. As temperatures and densities of deep and shallow waters change with the warming of spring, another turnover may occur. However, in most cases the lakes remain mixed throughout the winter.

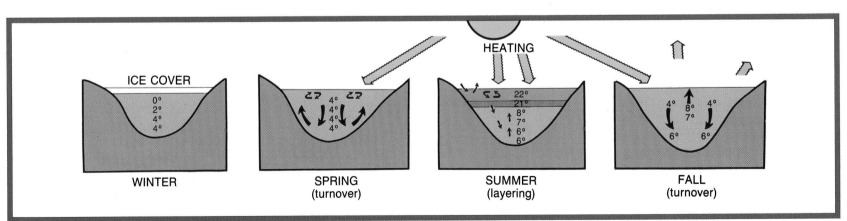

LAKE STRATIFICATION (LAYERING) AND TURNOVER. Heat from the sun and changing seasons cause water in large lakes to stratify or form layers. In winter, the ice cover stays at 0° C (32° F) and the water remains warmer below the ice than in the air above. Water is most dense at 4° C (39° F). In the spring turnover, warmer water rises as the surface heats up. In fall, surface waters cool, become denser and descend as heat is lost from the surface. In summer, stratification is caused by a warming of surface waters, which form a distinct layer called the epilimnion. This is separated from the cooler and denser waters of the hypolimnion by the thermocline, a layer of rapid temperature transition. Turnover distributes oxygen annually throughout most of the lakes.

Layering of lake water as it warms in summer can prevent the dispersion of effluents from tributaries, causing increased concentration of pollutants near the shore.

LIVING RESOURCES

As an ecosystem, the Great Lakes basin is a unit of nature in which living organisms and nonliving things interact adaptively. An ecosystem is fueled by the sun, which provides energy in the form of light and heat. This energy warms the earth, the water and the air, causing winds, currents, evaporation and precipitation. The light energy of the sun is essential for the photosynthesis of green plants in water and on land. Plants grow when essential nutrients such as phosphorus and nitrogen are present with oxygen, inorganic carbon and adequate water.

Plant material is consumed in the water by zooplankton, which graze the waters for algae, and on land by plant-eating animals (herbivores). Next in the chain of energy transfer through the ecosystem are organisms that feed on other animals (carnivores) and those that feed on both animals and plants (omnivores). Together these levels of consumption constitute the food chain, or web, a system of energy transfers through which an ecological community consisting of a complex of species is sustained. The population of each species is determined by a system of checks and balances based on factors such as the availability of food and the presence of predators, including disease organisms.

Every ecosystem also includes numerous processes to break down accumulated biomass (plants, animals and their wastes) into the constituent materials and nutrients from which they originated. Decomposition involves micro-organisms that are essential to the ecosystem because they recycle matter that can be used again.

Stable ecosystems are sustained by the interactions that cycle nutrients and energy in a balance between available resources and the life that depends on those resources. In ecosystems, including the Great Lakes basin, everything depends on everything else and nothing is ever really wasted.

The ecosystem of the Great Lakes and the life supported within it have continuously altered with time. Through periods of climate change and glaciation, species moved in and out of the region; some perished and others pioneered under changed circumstances. None of the changes, however, has been as rapid as that which occurred with the arrival of European settlers.

When the first Europeans arrived in the basin nearly 400 years ago, it was a lush, thickly vegetated area. Vast timber stands, consisting of oaks, maples and other hardwoods dominated the southern areas. Only a very few small vestiges of the original forest remain today. Between the wooded areas were rich grasslands with growth as high as 2 or 3 metres (7 to 10 feet). In the north, coniferous forests occupied the shallow, sandy soils, interspersed by bogs and other wetlands.

The forest and grasslands supported a wide variety of life, such as moose in the wetlands and coniferous woods, and deer in the grasslands and brush forests of the south. The many waterways and wetlands were home to beaver and muskrat which, with the fox, wolf and other fur-bearing species,

The layering and turnover of water annually are important for water quality. Turnover is the main way in which oxygen-poor water in the deeper areas of the lakes can be mixed with surface water containing more dissolved oxygen. This prevents anoxia, or complete oxygen depletion, of the lower levels of most of the lakes. However, the process of stratification during the summer also tends to restrict dilution of pollutants from effluents and land runoff.

During the spring warming period, the rapidly warming nearshore waters are inhibited from moving to the open lake by a thermal bar, a sharp temperature gradient that prevents mixing until the sun warms the open lake surface waters or until the waters are mixed by storms. Because the thermal bar holds pollutants nearshore, they are not dispersed to the open waters and can become more concentrated within the nearshore areas.

Double-crested Cormorants occupy an island in Lake Erie.

inhabited the mature forest lands. These were trapped and traded as commodities by the native people and the Europeans. Abundant bird populations thrived on the various terrains, some migrating to the south in winter, others making permanent homes in the basin.

It is estimated that there were as many as 180 species of fish indigenous to the Great Lakes. Those inhabiting the nearshore areas included smallmouth and largemouth bass, muskellunge, northern pike and channel catfish. In the open water were lake herring, blue pike, lake whitefish, walleye, sauger, freshwater drum, lake trout and white bass. Because of the differences in the characteristics of the lakes, the species composition varied for each of the Great Lakes. Warm, shallow Lake Erie was the most productive, while deep Superior was the least productive.

Changes in the species composition of the Great Lakes basin in the last 200 years have been the result of human activities. Many native fish species have been lost by overfishing, habitat destruction or the arrival of exotic or non-indigenous species, such as the lamprey and the alewife. Pollution, especially in the form of nutrient loading and toxic contaminants, has placed additional stresses on fish populations. Other human-made stresses have altered reproductive conditions and habitats, causing some varieties to migrate or perish. Still other effects on lake life result from damming, canal building, altering or polluting tributaries to the lakes in which spawning takes place and where distinct ecosystems once thrived and contributed to the larger basin ecosystem.

The FOOD WEB is a simplified way of understanding the process by which organisms in higher trophic levels gain energy by consuming organisms at lower trophic levels. All energy in an ecosystem originates with the sun. The solar energy is transformed by green plants through a process of photosynthesis into stored chemical energy. This is consumed by plant-eating animals, which are in turn consumed as food. Humans are part of the food web. The concept of the food web explains how some persistent contaminants accumulate in an ecosystem and become biologically magnified (see biomagnification and bioaccumulation in Chapter Four).

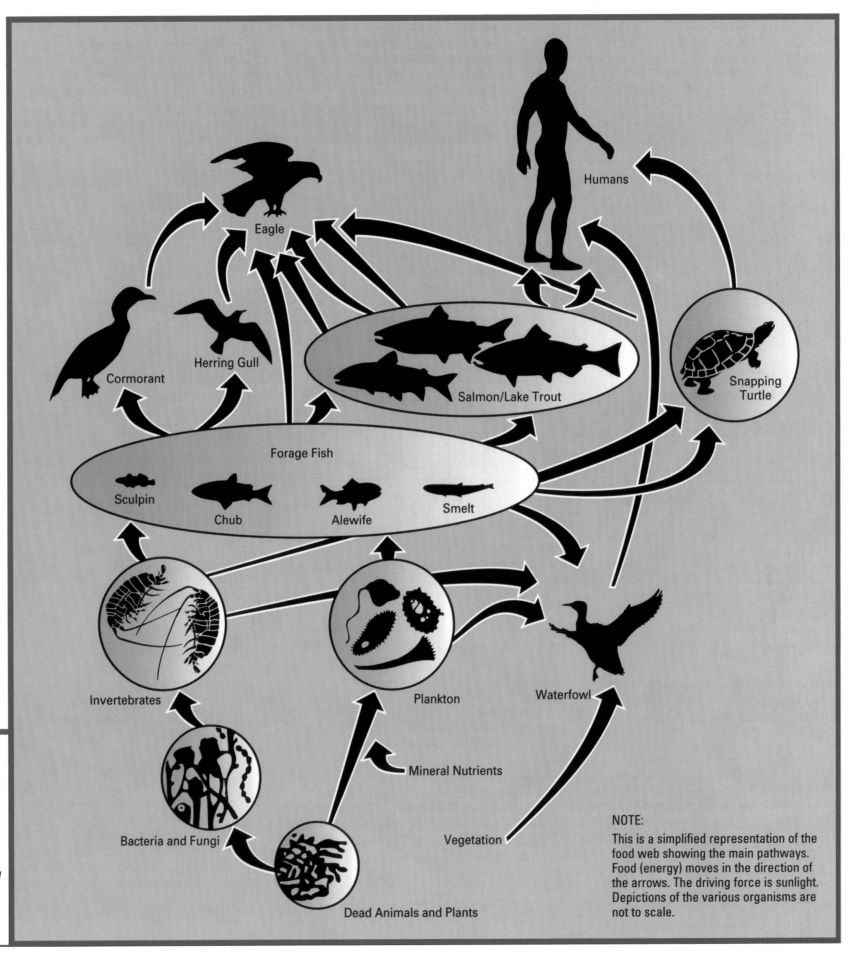

NOTE:
This is a simplified representation of the food web showing the main pathways. Food (energy) moves in the direction of the arrows. The driving force is sunlight. Depictions of the various organisms are not to scale.

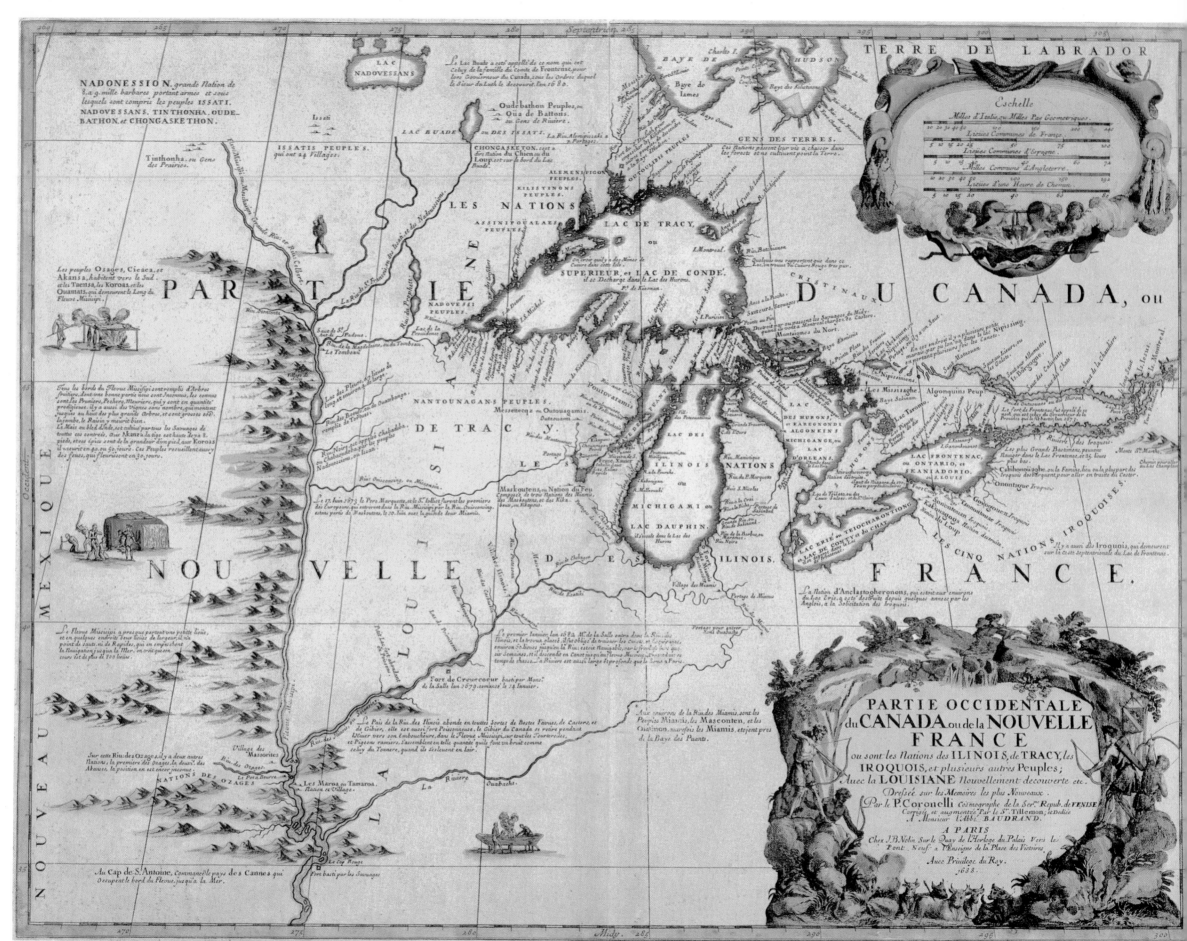

Coronelli's 1688 Map of Western New France. The first printed map to show the Great Lakes in their entirety and the most accurate general portrayal of the lakes and tributaries in the 17th century.

NATIVE PEOPLE

The first inhabitants of the Great Lakes basin arrived about 10,000 years ago. They had crossed the land bridge from Asia or perhaps had reached South America across the vastness of the Pacific Ocean. Six thousand years ago, descendants of the first settlers were using copper from the south shore of Lake Superior and had established hunting and fishing communities throughout the Great Lakes basin.

The population in the Great Lakes area is estimated to have been between 60,000 and 117,000 in the 16th century, when Europeans began their search for a passage to the Orient through the Great Lakes. The native people occupied widely scattered villages and grew corn, squash, beans and tobacco. They moved once or twice in a generation, when the resources in an area became exhausted.

EARLY SETTLEMENT BY EUROPEANS

By the early 1600s, the French had explored the forests around the St. Lawrence Valley and had begun to exploit the area for furs. The first area of the lakes to be visited by Europeans was Georgian Bay, reached via the Ottawa River and Lake Nipissing by the explorer Samuel de Champlain or perhaps Étienne Brulé, one of Champlain's scouts, in 1615. To the south and east, the Dutch and English began to settle on the eastern seaboard of what is now the United States. Although a confederacy of five Indian nations confined European settlement to the area east of the Appalachians, the French were able to establish bases in the lower St. Lawrence Valley. This enabled them to penetrate into the heart of the continent via the Ottawa River. In 1670, the French built the first of a chain of Great Lakes forts to protect the fur trade near the Mission of St. Ignace at the Straits of Mackinac. In 1673, Fort Frontenac, on the present site of Kingston, Ontario, became the first fort on the lower lakes.

Through the 17th century precious furs were transported to Hochelaga (Montreal) on the Great Lakes routes, but no permanent European settlements were maintained except at Forts Frontenac, Michilimackinac and Niagara. After Fort Oswego was established on the south shore of Lake Ontario by the

PEOPLE
and the
GREAT LAKES

Native people were the first to use the many resources of the Great Lakes basin. Abundant game, fertile soils and plentiful water enabled the early development of hunting, subsistence agriculture and fishing. The lakes and tributaries provided convenient transportation by canoe, and trade among groups flourished.

British in 1727, settlement was encouraged in the Mohawk and other valleys leading toward the lakes. A showdown between the British and the French for control of the Great Lakes ended with the British capture of Quebec in 1759.

The British maintained control of the Great Lakes during the American Revolution and, at the close of the conflict, the Great Lakes became the boundary between the new U.S. republic and what remained of British North America. The British granted land to the Loyalists who fled the former New England colonies to Upper and Lower Canada, now the southern regions of the provinces of Ontario and Quebec, respectively. Between

1792 and 1800 the population of Upper Canada increased from 20,000 to 60,000. The new American government also moved to develop the Great Lakes region with the passage by Congress of the Ordinance of 1787. This legislation covered everything from land sale to provisions for statehood for the Northwest Territory, the area between the Great Lakes and the Ohio River west of Pennsylvania.

The final military challenge for the wealth of the Great Lakes region came with the War of 1812. For the Americans, the war was about the expansion into, and development of, the area around the lakes. For the British, it meant the defense of its remaining imperial holdings in North America. The war proved to be a short one – only 2 years – but final. When the shooting was over both the Americans and the British claimed victory.

Canada had survived invasion and was set on an inevitable course to nationhood. The new American nation had failed to conquer Upper Canada but gained needed national confidence and prestige. Native people, who had become involved in the war in order to secure a homeland, did not share in the victory. The winners in the War of 1812 were those who dreamed of settling the Great Lakes region. The long-awaited development of the area from a beautiful, almost uninhabited wilderness into a home and workplace for millions began in earnest.

DEVELOPMENT OF THE LAKES

During the next 150 years the development of the Great Lakes basin proceeded with haste. The battles for territory so common during the era of empires and colonies gave way to nation-building, city-building and industrialization. The warriors of the previous era gave way to, or themselves became, the entrepreneurs, farmers and laborers who ran the mills, tilled the soil and provided the skills and services required for modern industrial economies.

The development of the Great Lakes region proceeded along several lines that took advantage of the many resources within the basin. The waterways became major highways of trade and were exploited for

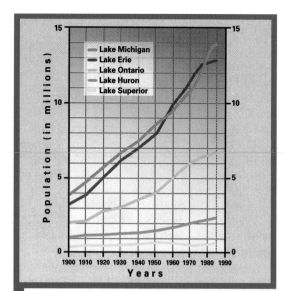

Population growth in the Great Lakes basin since 1900.

their fish. The fertile land that had provided the original wealth of furs and food yielded lumber, then wheat, then other agricultural products. Bulk goods such as iron ore and coal were shipped through Great Lakes ports, and manufacturing grew.

AGRICULTURE

The promise of agricultural land was the greatest attraction to the immigrants to the Great Lakes region in the 19th century. By the mid-1800s, most of the Great Lakes region where farming was possible was settled. The population had swelled tremendously. There were about 400,000 people in Michigan, 300,000 in Wisconsin and perhaps half a million in Upper Canada.

Canals led to broader commodity export opportunities, allowing farmers to expand their operations beyond a subsistence level. Wheat and corn were the first commodities to be packed in barrels and shipped abroad. Grist mills – one of the region's first industries – were built on the tributaries flowing into the lakes to process the grains for overseas markets.

As populations grew, dairying and meat production for local consumption began to dominate agriculture in the Great Lakes basin. Specialty crops, such as fruit, vegetables and tobacco, grown for the burgeoning urban population, claimed an increasingly important share of the lands suitable for them.

The rapid, large-scale clearing of land for agriculture brought rapid changes in the ecosystem. Soils stripped of vegetation washed away to the lakes; tributaries and silty deltas clogged and altered the flow of the rivers. Fish habitats and spawning areas were destroyed. Greater surface runoff led to increased seasonal fluctuation in water levels and the creation of more flood-prone lands along the waterway. Agricultural development has also contributed to Great Lakes pollution, chiefly in the form of eutrophication. Fertilizers that reach waterways in soils and runoff stimulate growth of algae and other water plants. The plants die and decay, depleting the oxygen in the water. Lack of oxygen leads to fish kills, and the character of the ecosystem changes as the original plants and animals give way to more pollution-tolerant species.

Modern row crop monoculture relies heavily on chemicals to control pests such as insects, fungi and weeds. These chemicals are usually synthetic organic substances and they find their way to rivers and lakes to affect plant and animal life, and threaten human health. The problem was first recognized with DDT, a very persistent chemical, which tended to remain in the environment for a long time and to bioaccumulate through the food chain. It caused reproductive failures in some species of birds. Since the use of DDT was banned, some bird populations are now recovering. Other, less persistent, chemicals have replaced DDT and other problem pesticides, but toxic contamination from agricultural practices continues to be a concern. DDT levels in fish are declining but, in spite of being banned, some other pesticides, such as dieldrin, continue to persist in fish at relatively high levels.

LOGGING AND FORESTRY

The original logging operations in the Great Lakes basin involved clearing the land for agriculture and building houses and barns for the settlers. Much of the wood was simply burned. By the 1830s, however, commercial logging began in Upper Canada. A few years later logging began in Michigan, and operations in Minnesota and Wisconsin soon followed.

Once again the lakes played a vital role. Cutting was generally done in the winter months by men from the farms. They traveled up the rivers felling trees that were floated down to the lakes during the spring thaw. The logs were formed into huge rafts or loosely gathered in booms to be towed by steam tugs. This latter practice had to be stopped because logs often escaped the boom and seriously interfered with shipping. In time, timber was carried in ships specially designed for log transport.

The earliest loggers mainly harvested white pine. In virgin stands these trees reached 60 metres (200 feet) in height, and a single tree could contain 10 cubic metres (6,000 board feet) of lumber. It was light and strong and much in demand for shipbuilding and construction. Each year, loggers had to move farther west and north in search of white pine. The trees were hundreds of years old and so were not soon replaced. When the resource was exhausted, lumbermen had to utilize other species. The hardwoods such as maple, walnut and oak were cut to make furniture, barrels and specialty products.

Paper-making from pulpwood developed slowly. The first sulfite process paper mill was built on the Welland Canal in the 1860s. Paper production developed at Green Bay in the U.S. and elsewhere in the Great Lakes basin. Eventually Canada and the U.S. became the world's leading producers of pulp and paper products. Today much of this production still occurs in the Great Lakes area. The pulp and paper industry (along with chloralkali production) contributed to the mercury pollution problem on the Great Lakes until the early 1970s, when mercury was banned from use in the industry.

The logging industry was exploitive during its early stages. Huge stands were lost in fires, often because of poor management of litter from logging operations. In Canada, lumbering was largely done on crown lands with a small tax charged per tree. In the United States, cutting was done on private land but when it was cleared, the owners often stopped paying taxes and let the land revert to public ownership. In both cases, clear-cutting was the usual practice. Without proper rehabilitation of the forest, soils were readily eroded from barren landscapes and lost to local streams, rivers and lakes. In some areas of the Great Lakes basin, reforestation has not been adequate and today, as a result, the forests may be a diminishing resource.

Great Lakes Factsheet No. 2 Land And Shoreline Uses

	Superior %	Michigan %	Huron %	Erie %	Ontario %
BASIN LAND USE					
Agricultural					
Canada	0.5		21	80	49
U.S.	6.0	44	40	63	33
Total	3.0	44	27	67	39
Residential					
Canada	0.1		1	4	6
U.S.	3.0	9	6	12	8
Total	1.0	9	2	10	7
Forest					
Canada	98.7		75	15	42
U.S.	80.0	41	52	23	53
Total	91.0	41	68	21	49
Other					
Canada	0.7		3	1	3
U.S.	11.0	6	2	2	6
Other	5.0	6	3	1	5
SHORELINE USE					
Residential					
Canada	n/a		34	39	25
U.S.		39	42	45	40
Recreational					
Canada	n/a		8	8	15
U.S.		24	4	13	12
Agricultural					
Canada	n/a		4	21	30
U.S.		20	15	14	33
Commercial					
Canada	n/a		35	10	18
U.S.		12	32	12	8
Other					
Canada	n/a		19	22	12
U.S.		5	7	16	7

Source: BULLETINS E-1866-70, Sea Grant College Program, Cooperative Extension Service, Michigan State University, E. Lansing, Michigan, 1985.

n/a: not available

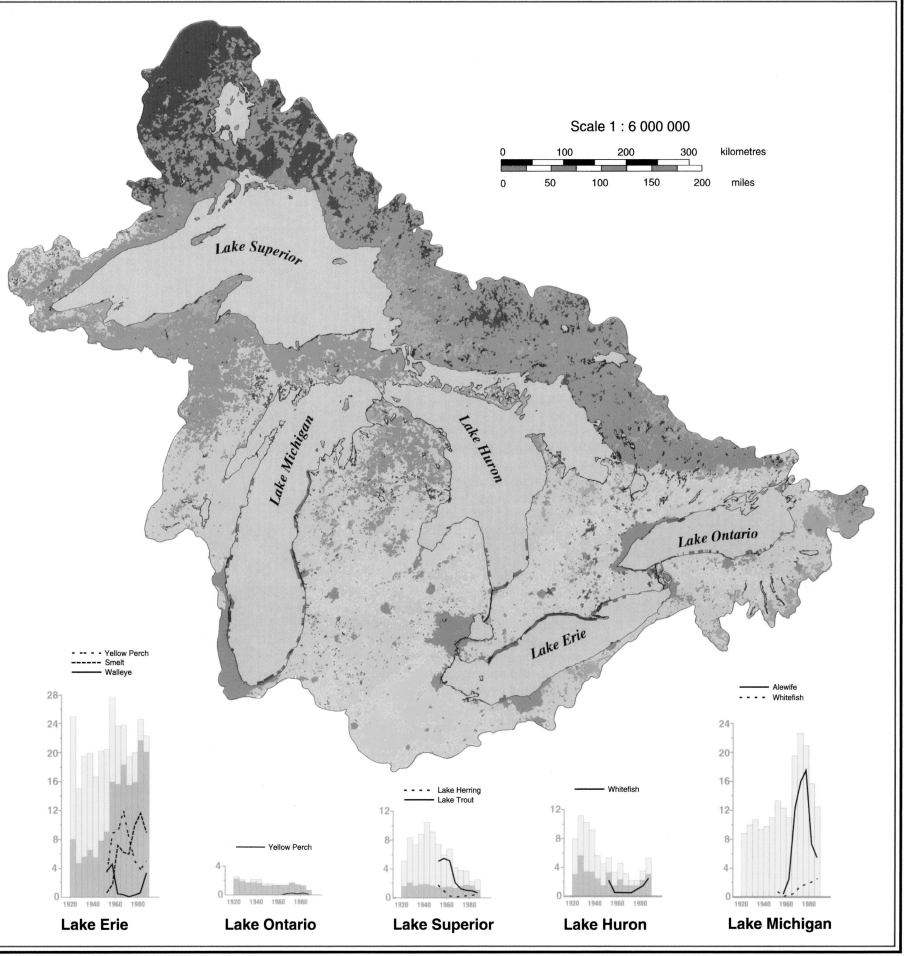

LAND USE, FISHERIES & EROSION

LAND USE

- Intensive General Farming
- Low-intensity Farming/Pasture
- Coniferous Forest
- Mixed-wood Forest
- Deciduous Forest
- Urban Areas

COMMERCIAL FISHERIES

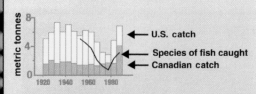

← U.S. catch
← Species of fish caught
← Canadian catch

NOTE:

1. Each bar represents the average catch over a five-year period.

2. The species shown for each lake are those which have been consistently important since 1950. They are not necessarily those which yielded the largest catch in any five-year period.

	Tonnes	Tons
	4 000	4 400
	8 000	8 825
	12 000	13 225
	16 000	17 625
	20 000	22 050
	24 000	26 450
	28 000	30 875

SHORELINE EROSION

- Minimal
- Moderate
- Severe

Scale 1 : 6 000 000

Lake Superior

Lake Michigan

Lake Huron

Lake Ontario

Lake Erie

---- Yellow Perch
- - - - Smelt
——— Walleye

Lake Erie

——— Yellow Perch

Lake Ontario

- - - - Lake Herring
——— Lake Trout

Lake Superior

——— Whitefish

Lake Huron

——— Alewife
---- Whitefish

Lake Michigan

Geomatics International Cartography

A Great Lakes freighter passes through the Welland Canal linking Lakes Erie and Ontario.

CANALS, SHIPPING AND TRANSPORTATION

Conflict over the Great Lakes continued after the War of 1812 in the form of competition to improve transportation routes. By 1825, the 586 km (364 mile) Erie Canal, a waterway from Albany, New York, to Buffalo, was carrying settlers west and freight east. The cost of goods in the west fell 90 percent while the price of agricultural products shipped through the lakes rose dramatically. Settlement in the fertile expanses of Ohio and Michigan became even more attractive.

The Canadians opened the Lachine Canal at about the same time to bypass the worst rapids on the St. Lawrence River. In 1829, the Welland Canal joined Lakes Erie and Ontario, bypassing Niagara Falls. Other canals linked the Great Lakes to the Ohio and Mississippi Rivers, and the Great Lakes became the hub of transportation in eastern North America.

Railroads replaced the canals after mid-century, making still-important transportation links between the Great Lakes and both seacoasts. In 1959, completion of the St.

Lawrence Seaway allowed modern ocean vessels to enter the lakes, but shipping has not expanded as much as expected because of intense competition from other modes of transportation such as trucking and railroads.

Today, the three main commodities shipped on the Great Lakes are iron ore, coal and grain. Transport of iron ore has declined as some steel mills in the region have shut down or reduced production, but steel-making capacity in North America is likely to remain concentrated in the Great Lakes region. Coal moves both east and west within the lakes, but coal export abroad has not expanded as much as was anticipated during the rapid rise of oil prices in the 1970s. As a result of economic decline, the Great Lakes fleet of over 300 vessels is being reduced through the retirement of the older, smaller vessels.

COMMERCIAL FISHERIES

Fish were important as food for the region's native people, as well as for the first European settlers. Commercial fishing began about 1820 and expanded about 20 percent per year. The largest Great Lakes fish harvests were recorded in 1889 and 1899 at some 67,000 tonnes (147 million pounds). However, by the 1880s some preferred species in Lake Erie had declined. Catches increased with more efficient fishing equipment but the golden days of the commercial fishery were over by the late 1950s. Since then, average annual catches have been around 50,000 tonnes (110 million pounds). The value of the commercial fishery has declined drastically because the more valuable, larger fish have given way to small and relatively low-value species. Over-fishing, pollution, shoreline and stream habitat destruction, and accidental and deliberate introduction of exotic species such as the sea lamprey all played a part in the decline of the fishery.

Today, lake trout, sturgeon and lake herring survive in vastly reduced numbers and have been replaced by introduced species such as smelt, alewife, splake, and Pacific salmon. Populations of some of the native species such as yellow perch, walleye and white bass have made good recovery. Lake trout, once the top predator in the lakes, survives in sufficient numbers to allow commercial fishing only in Lake

Superior, the only lake where substantial natural reproduction still occurs. However, even in Superior, hatchery-reared trout are stocked annually to maintain the population.

In addition to the lake trout, the blue pike of Lake Erie, and the Atlantic salmon of Lake Ontario were top predators in the open waters of the lakes and were major components of the commercial fishery in earlier times. Of the three, the blue pike and Lake Ontario Atlantic salmon are believed to be extinct. Currently, hatchery-reared coho and chinook salmon are the most plentiful top predators in the open lakes except in the western portion of Lake Erie, which is dominated by walleye.

Only pockets remain of the once large commercial fishery. The Canadian commercial fishery in Lake Erie remains prosperous. In 1991, 750 Canadian fishermen harvested a total of about 2,300 tonnes (50 million pounds) with a landed value of about $59 million (Canadian). For Canada, the Lake Erie fishery represents nearly two-thirds of the total Great Lakes harvest. All commercial fish caught in

Canada are inspected prior to market for quality and compliance with federal regulations.

In the United States, the commercial fishery is based on lake whitefish, smelt, bloater chubs and perch, and on alewife for animal feed. Commercial fishing is limited by a federal prohibition on the sale of fish affected by toxic contaminants. Pressure to limit commercial fishing in the U.S. is also exerted by sport fishing groups anxious to manage the fishery in their interests. In addition, the trend in the U.S. is to reduce the pressure on the fishery by restricting commercial fishing to trapnets that harvest species selectively, without killing species preferred by recreational fishermen.

Commercial fishing is under continuing pressure from several fronts. Toxic contaminants could cause the closure of additional fisheries as the ability to measure the presence of chemicals improves together with the knowledge of their effects on human health.

The commercial fishery prospers in a few locations on the lakes. Above, Lake Erie fishermen out of Port Dover, Ontario harvest a trawl net of smelt.

WATERBORNE COMMERCE

CARGO VOLUME BY PORT IN TONNES, 1990

Ports under 2 500 000 tonnes

- ○ 100 000 - 500 000 tonnes
- ○ 500 000 - 2 500 000 tonnes
- ● Ports over 2 500 000 tonnes

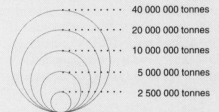

- 40 000 000 tonnes
- 20 000 000 tonnes
- 10 000 000 tonnes
- 5 000 000 tonnes
- 2 500 000 tonnes

COMMODITY TYPES

- Coal
- Grains/Soybeans
- Iron Ore
- Cement
- Chemicals
- Coke
- Electrical Products
- Limestone
- Metals and Metal Products
- Petroleum Products
- Other

INTER-LAKE COMMODITY FLOW IN TONNES, 1990

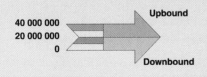

40 000 000   Upbound

20 000 000

0

Downbound

Tonnes	Tons
1 000	1 100
100 000	110 250
500 000	551 270
2 500 000	2 756 340
5 000 000	5 512 680
10 000 000	11 025 360
20 000 000	22 050 720
30 000 000	33 076 070
40 000 000	44 101 430

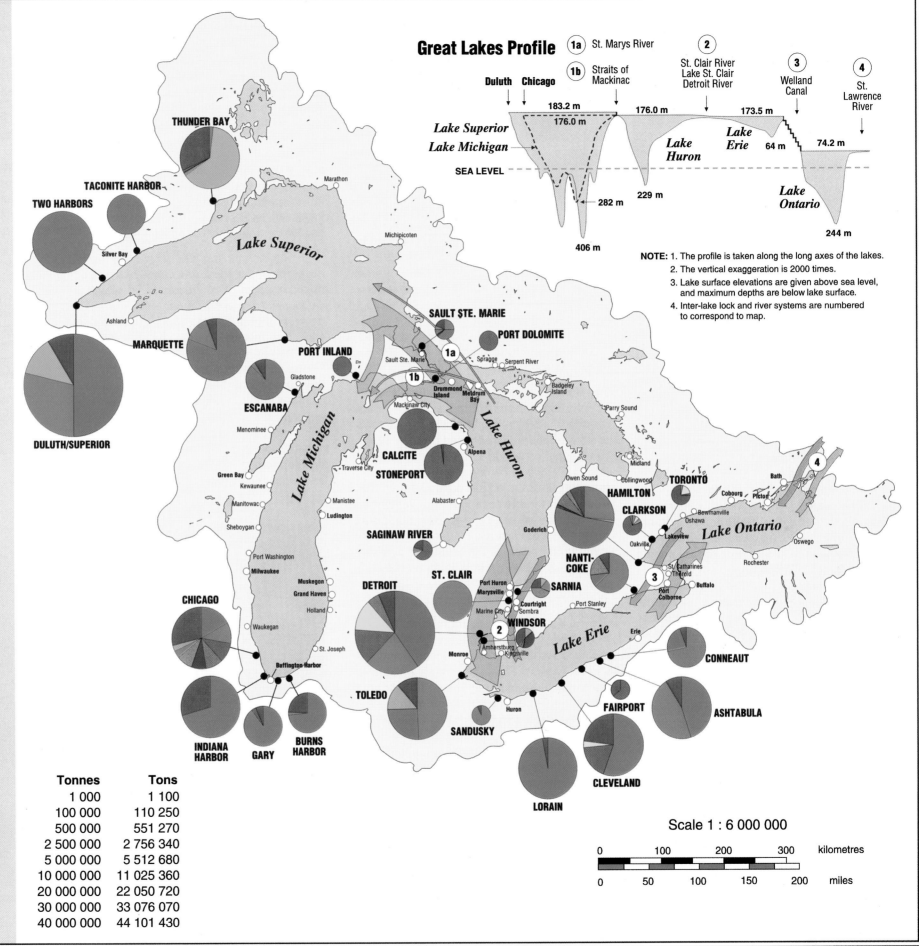

Great Lakes Profile

1a St. Marys River
1b Straits of Mackinac
2 St. Clair River / Lake St. Clair / Detroit River
3 Welland Canal
4 St. Lawrence River

Duluth   Chicago

Lake Superior / Lake Michigan

183.2 m   176.0 m   176.0 m   173.5 m

Lake Huron   Lake Erie   64 m   74.2 m

SEA LEVEL

282 m   229 m   Lake Ontario

406 m   244 m

NOTE:
1. The profile is taken along the long axes of the lakes.
2. The vertical exaggeration is 2000 times.
3. Lake surface elevations are given above sea level, and maximum depths are below lake surface.
4. Inter-lake lock and river systems are numbered to correspond to map.

Scale 1 : 6 000 000

| 0 | 100 | 200 | 300 | kilometres |
| 0 | 50 | 100 | 150 | 200 | miles |

The development of pleasure-boat marinas is one of the recreational activities that has increased in recent years, often placing pressure on the shoreline.

Sport Fishery

Several factors have contributed to the success of the sport fisheries. The sea lamprey, which almost destroyed the lake trout population, is being successfully controlled using chemical lampricides and low-head barrier dams. Walleye populations rebounded in Lake Erie owing to regulation of the commercial fishery and improvements in water quality. The population of alewife exploded as lamprey destroyed native top predators. The increase in alewife provided a forage base for new predators such as coho and chinook salmon, which were introduced in the 1960s to fill the gap left by depleted lake trout stocks, when lamprey populations declined.

The sport fishery developed quickly as Pacific salmon rapidly grew to large sizes after they were introduced into Lake Michigan. Charter fleets developed and a minor tourist boom led to plans to develop a large fish stocking program to fuel a new sport fishing industry.

By 1980, the idea of stocking exotic fish such as salmon to support the sport fishery had spread to all the lakes and jurisdictions. Ontario and Michigan also experimented with the 'splake', a hybrid of the native lake trout and brook (or speckled) trout. None of these predators has been able to reproduce very well, if at all, so the fishery has been maintained by stocking year after year. Ironically, the exception is the pink salmon, a small species accidentally introduced into Lake Superior in 1955. It has survived to establish spawning populations and spread through Lakes Michigan and Huron, where it established self-propagating populations by the 1980s.

Recreation

Since early in the industrial age, the waterways, shorelines and woodlands of the Great Lakes region have been attractions for leisure time activities. Many of the utilitarian activities that were so important in the early settlement and industrial development became recreational activities in later years. For example, boating, fishing and canoeing were once commercial activities, but are now primarily leisure pursuits.

Recreation in the area became an important economic and social activity with the age of travel in the 19th century. A thriving pleasure-boat industry based on the newly constructed canals developed, bringing people into the region in conjunction with rail and road travel. Niagara Falls attracted travelers from considerable distances and was one of the first stimulants to the growth of a leisure-related economy. Later, the reputation of the lower lakes region as the frontier of a pristine wilderness drew people seeking restful cures and miracle waters to the many spas and 'clinics' that developed along the waterway.

In the 20th century, more people had more free time. With industrial growth, greater personal disposable income and shorter work weeks, people of all walks of life began to spend their leisure time beyond the city limits. Governments on both sides of the border acquired lands and began to develop an extensive system of parks, wilderness areas and conservation areas in order to protect valuable local resources and to serve the needs of the population for recreation areas. Unfortunately, by the time the need for publicly accessible recreation lands had become apparent, much of the land in the basin, including virtually all the shoreline on the lower lakes, was in private hands. Today, about 80 percent of the U.S. shoreline and 20 percent of the Canadian shore is privately owned and not accessible by the public.

The recreation industry includes production and sale of sports equipment and boats, marinas, resorts, restaurants and related service industries that cater to a wide range of recreational activities. In some areas of the basin, recreation and tourism are becoming an increasingly important component of the economy, in place of manufacturing. The Great Lakes basin provides a wide range of recreational opportunities, ranging from pristine wilderness activities in national parks such as Isle Royale and Pukaskwa to intensive urban waterfront beaches in major urban areas.

The increasingly intensive recreational development of the Great Lakes has had mixed impacts. Some recreational activities cause environmental damage. Extensive development of cottage areas, summer home sites, beaches and marinas has resulted in loss of wetland, dune and forest areas. Shoreline alteration by developers and individual property owners has caused changes in the shoreline erosion and deposition process, often to the detriment of important beach and wetland systems that depend upon these processes. The development of areas susceptible to flooding and erosion has caused considerable public reaction. There is pressure to manage lake levels to prevent changes that are part of natural weather patterns and processes. Pollution from recreational sites and boats has also caused water-quality degradation.

Recreational uses are a threat to the quality of the Great Lakes ecosystem, but also provide a basis for protecting quality by attracting and involving people who recognize that protection of the ecosystem is essential to sustain the recreation that they value. People who use the water for its fun and beauty can become a potent force in the protection of the ecosystem. Naturalists, anglers and cottagers were among the first to bring environmental issues to the attention of the public and call for the cleanup of the lakes in the 1950s and 1960s, when eutrophication threatened favored fishing, bathing and wildlife sites. Today more people than ever use and value the lakes for recreational purposes.

Recent years have seen a major resurgence in recreational fishing as the walleye fisheries recover and the new salmon fisheries develop. Lake Ontario now sports a very important salmon and trout recreational fishery. The water-quality recovery in Lake Erie

The sandy beaches of the lower lakes provide one of the most popular summer recreational activities on the lakes.

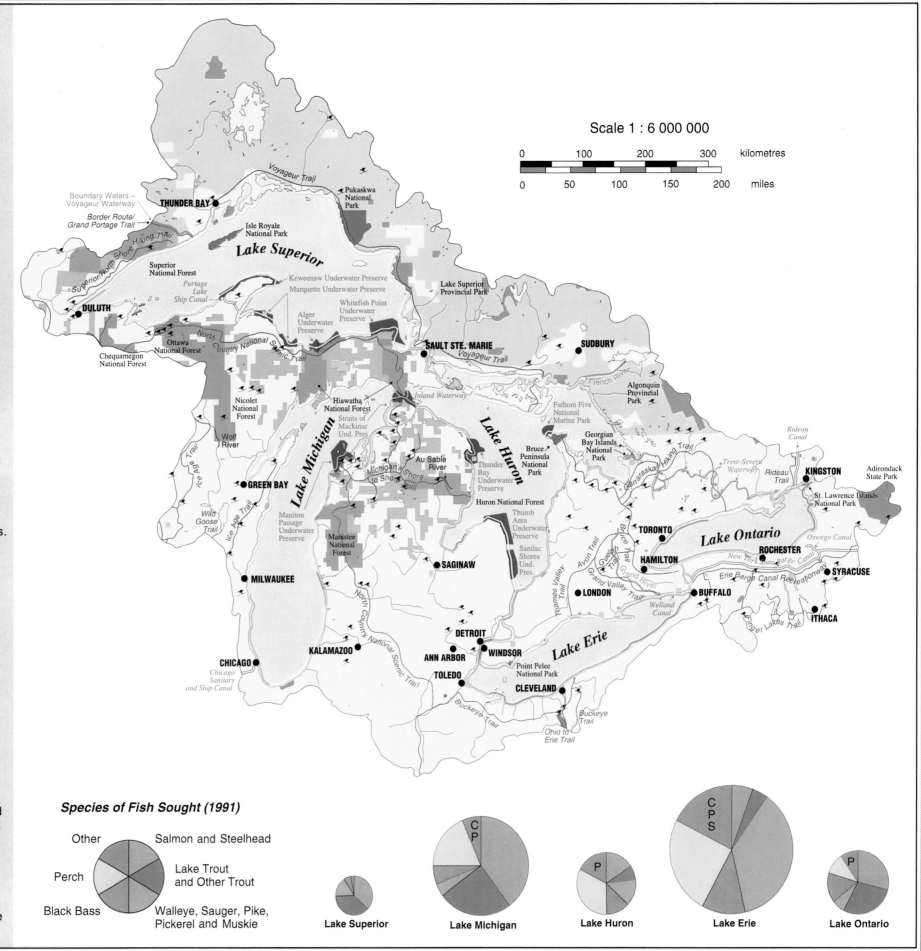

RECREATION

PROTECTED AREAS

- National Park
- State/Provincial Park
- National Forest
- State Forest
- National Lakeshore
- National Wildlife Area
- National Recreation Area
- National Marine Park/Underwater Preserve
- Crown Land

RECREATIONAL AREAS & ROUTES

- Ski Area
- Canoe Route
- Long-distance Trail
- Canalized Waterway
- Heritage River
- Scenic River

NOTE: 1. The canoe routes include portages.
2. Not all sections of the trails shown are yet in existence.

Recreational Boating Facilities

- Sparse
- Moderate
- Dense

SPORT FISHING

1. Area of circles are proportional to the number of angler days in 1991:
   Lake Superior –   883 000
   Lake Michigan – 5 090 000
   Lake Huron –   2 113 000
   Lake Erie –   7 082 000
   Lake Ontario –   2 394 000

2. The data measure sport fishing effort, and are classified according to species sought as opposed to species actually caught.

3. Significant species in the 'other' category are C – Catfish and bullhead, P – Panfish and S – Sheephead.

4. The 'other' category also includes those cases where the angler has no preference for the species caught.

Scale 1 : 6 000 000

0   100   200   300 kilometres

0   50   100   150   200 miles

Species of Fish Sought (1991)

Other — Salmon and Steelhead
Perch — Lake Trout and Other Trout
Black Bass — Walleye, Sauger, Pike, Pickerel and Muskie

Lake Superior

Lake Michigan

Lake Huron

Lake Erie

Lake Ontario

Geomatics International Cartography

has been complemented by record walleye reproduction in recent years. In many areas, Buffalo, Cleveland, Chicago and Toronto particularly, there have been urban renewal movements with the lake front as a primary focus. Developing public access to the water is a key element of these renewal projects.

URBANIZATION AND INDUSTRIAL GROWTH

Nearly all the settlements that grew into cities in the Great Lakes region were established on the waterways that transported people, raw materials and goods. The largest urban areas developed at the mouths of tributaries because of transportation advantages and the apparently inexhaustible supply of fresh water for domestic and industrial use. Historically, the major industries in the Great Lakes region have produced steel, paper, chemicals, automobiles and other manufactured goods.

A large part of the steel industry in Canada and the United States is concentrated in the Great Lakes because iron ore, coal and limestone can be carried on the lakes from mines and quarries to steel mills. In the United States, ore is carried from mines near Lake Superior to steel mills at the south end of Lake Michigan and at Detroit, Cleveland, and Lorain in the Lake Erie basin. In Canada, ore from the upper lakes region is processed in steel mills at Sault Ste. Marie, Hamilton and Nanticoke.

Paper-making in the U.S. occurs primarily on the upper lakes, with the largest concentration of mills along the Fox River, which feeds into Green Bay on Lake Michigan. In Canada, mills are located along the Welland Canal as well as along the upper lakes. Chemical industries developed on both sides of the Niagara River because of the availability of cheap electricity. Other major concentrations of chemical production are located near Saginaw Bay in Lake Huron and in Sarnia, Ontario, on the St. Clair River, because of abundant salt deposits and plentiful water.

All of these industrial activities produce vast quantities of wastes. Initially the wastes of urban-industrial centers did not appear to pose serious problems. Throughout most of the 19th century industrial wastes were dumped into the waterways, diluted and dispersed. Eventually, problems emerged when municipal water supplies became contaminated with urban-industrial effluent. The threat to public health from disease organisms prompted some cities to adopt practices that seemed for the time to solve the problem.

In 1854, Chicago experienced a cholera epidemic in which 5 percent of the population perished, and in 1891, the rate of death due to typhoid fever had reached a high of 124 per 100,000 population. To protect its drinking water supply from sewage, Chicago reversed the flow of the Chicago River away from Lake Michigan. A diversion channel was dug to carry sewage effluent away from Lake Michigan into the Illinois and Mississippi River system. In Hamilton, in the 1870s, water could no longer be drawn from the harbor or from local wells because of contamination. A steam-powered water pump was installed to draw deep water from Lake Ontario for distribution throughout the city.

Many of the dangers of industrial pollution to the Great Lakes and to human and environmental health were not recognized until recently, in part because their presence and their effects are difficult to detect. In recent years this has become especially evident where aging industrial disposal sites leak chemicals discarded many years ago into the environment or where sediments contaminated by long-standing industrial activities continue to contribute dangerous pollutants to the waterways. Now the region must cope with cleanup of the pollution from these past activities at the same time that the industrial base for the regional economy is struggling to remain competitive.

Use of Great Lakes resources brought wealth and well-being to the residents of Great Lakes cities but the full price of the concentration of industry and people is only now being understood. The cleanup of the Great Lakes region will require continuous expenditure by, and cooperation among, state, provincial and federal agencies, local governments and industry. Through this cooperation, combined with public involvement, contaminant levels in the Great Lakes ecosystem have declined dramatically since the 1970s. Because many pollutants tend to persist in the environment, levels must continue to be reduced. Pollution-prevention measures are being combined with cleanup to deal with pollution in the Great Lakes.

The City of Chicago on Lake Michigan is the largest urban area on the lakes.

The City of Toronto on Lake Ontario is the largest Canadian city on the lakes.

EMPLOYMENT & INDUSTRIAL STRUCTURE

POPULATION & EMPLOYMENT 1990 (USA) 1991 (CANADA)

Number of People

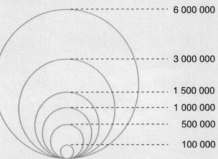

- 6 000 000
- 3 000 000
- 1 500 000
- 1 000 000
- 500 000
- 100 000

Employment Breakdown

Outer Circle = Total Population (TP)
Inner Circle = Working Population (WP)

INDUSTRIAL STRUCTURE, 1990 (USA) 1991 (CANADA)

Public Administration and Defense
Primary Industry (agriculture, forestry, mining)
Community Services (health, education, religion)
Construction
Personal Services (recreation, repairs, hotels, etc.)
Manufacturing Industry
Finance, Insurance, Real Estate
Transportation and Communications
Trade (retail and wholesale)

STATISTICAL AREAS

1. The data mapped are based on Census Metropolitan Areas (CMAs) in Canada and Metropolitan Statistical Areas (MSAs) in the United States, shown as:

2. In several cases, contiguous CMAs and MSAs have been combined to preserve clarity.

3. Note that certain MSAs extend beyond the watershed boundary of the Great Lakes basin.

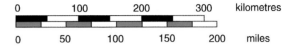

Scale 1 : 6 000 000

0 100 200 300 kilometres
0 50 100 150 200 miles

Lake Superior
Lake Michigan
Lake Huron
Lake Ontario
Lake Erie

1. Thunder Bay
TP: 124 427
WP: 65 155

2. Duluth
TP: 239 971
WP: 110 851

3. Appleton-Oshkosh-Neenah, Green Bay, Sheboygan
TP: 613 592
WP: 324 463

4. Milwaukee, Racine
TP: 1 607 185
WP: 873 809

5. Chicago, Kenosha, Lake County, Gary-Hammond
TP: 7 319 099
WP: 3 788 047

6. Elkhart-Goshen, South Bend-Mishawaka
TP: 403 250
WP: 208 193

7. Benton Harbor, Kalamazoo
TP: 384 789
WP: 197 365

8. Grand Rapids, Muskegon
TP: 847 382
WP: 434 055

9. Battle Creek, Jackson, Lansing-East Lansing
TP: 718 412
WP: 366 256

10. Flint, Saginaw-Bay City-Midland
TP: 829 779
WP: 389 814

11. Detroit-Ann Arbor
TP: 4 665 236
WP: 2 326 077

12. Windsor
TP: 262 421
WP: 130 745

13. Toledo
TP: 614 128
WP: 303 422

14. Fort Wayne
TP: 363 811
WP: 193 730

15. Lima
TP: 154 340
WP: 74 584

16. Cleveland, Akron, Lorain-Elyria
TP: 2 759 823
WP: 1 687 067

17. Erie
TP: 275 572
WP: 132 202

18. London
TP: 381 522
WP: 208 915

19. Sudbury
TP: 157 619
WP: 80 020

20. Kitchener
TP: 356 421
WP: 198 065

21. Toronto
TP: 3 893 046
WP: 2 195 550

22. Oshawa
TP: 240 104
WP: 130 225

23. Hamilton
TP: 599 760
WP: 318 330

24. St. Catharines, Niagara Falls
TP: 343 258
WP: 186 390

25. Buffalo, Niagara Falls
TP: 1 189 288
WP: 584 658

26. Rochester
TP: 1 002 410
WP: 519 059

27. Syracuse
TP: 659 864
WP: 332 361

Geomatics International Cartography

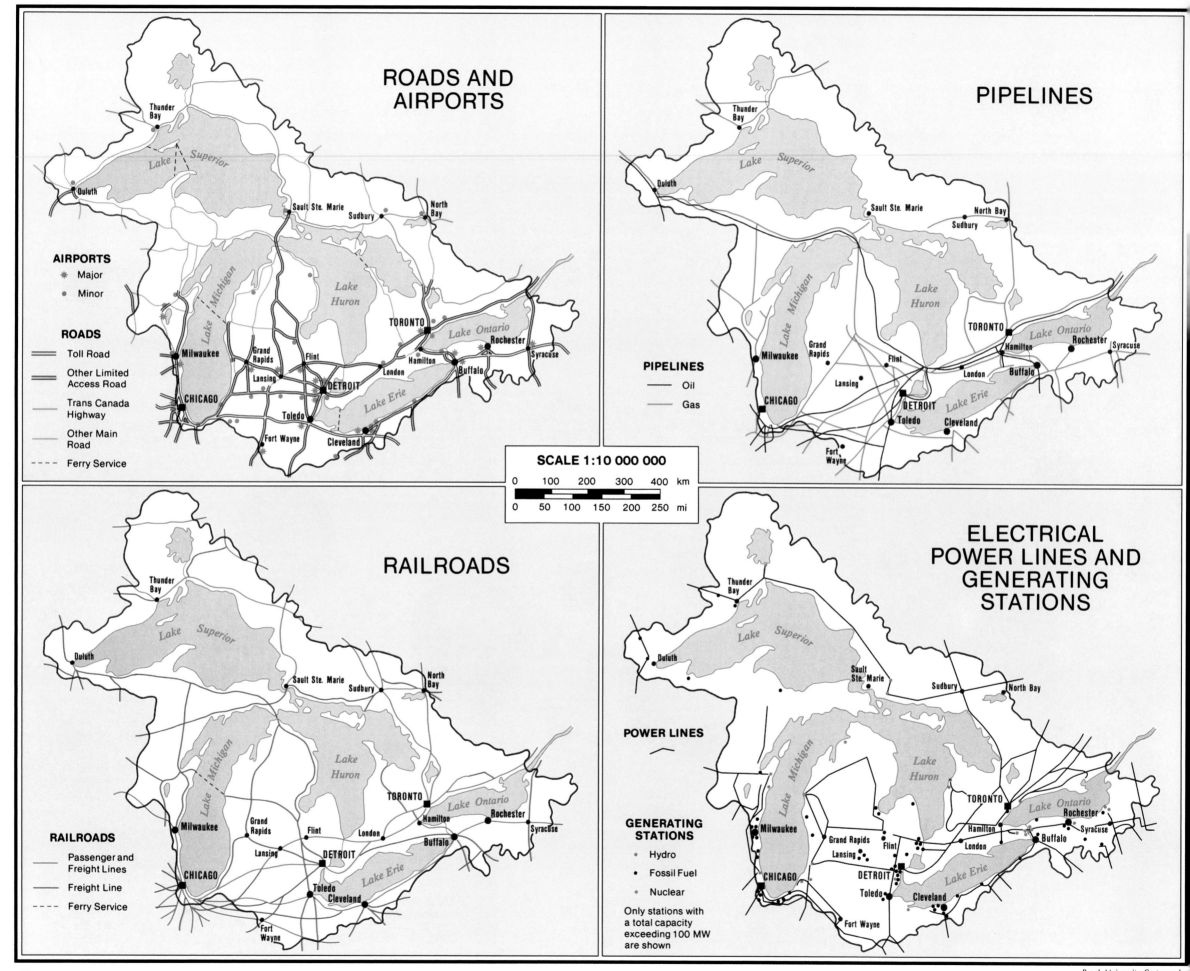

ROADS AND AIRPORTS

AIRPORTS
* Major
• Minor

ROADS
Toll Road
Other Limited Access Road
Trans Canada Highway
Other Main Road
Ferry Service

Thunder Bay
Duluth
Sault Ste. Marie
Sudbury
North Bay
TORONTO
Rochester
Syracuse
Hamilton
Buffalo
Milwaukee
London
Grand Rapids
Flint
Lansing
DETROIT
CHICAGO
Toledo
Fort Wayne
Cleveland

Lake Superior
Lake Michigan
Lake Huron
Lake Ontario
Lake Erie

PIPELINES

PIPELINES
Oil
Gas

Thunder Bay
Duluth
Sault Ste. Marie
North Bay
Sudbury
TORONTO
Rochester
Syracuse
Hamilton
Buffalo
Milwaukee
Grand Rapids
Flint
London
Lansing
DETROIT
Toledo
Cleveland
Fort Wayne
CHICAGO

Lake Superior
Lake Michigan
Lake Huron
Lake Ontario
Lake Erie

SCALE 1:10 000 000

0   100   200   300   400 km

0   50   100   150   200   250 mi

RAILROADS

RAILROADS
Passenger and Freight Lines
Freight Line
Ferry Service

Thunder Bay
Duluth
Sault Ste. Marie
Sudbury
North Bay
TORONTO
Rochester
Syracuse
Hamilton
Buffalo
Milwaukee
Grand Rapids
Flint
London
Lansing
DETROIT
CHICAGO
Toledo
Cleveland
Fort Wayne

Lake Superior
Lake Michigan
Lake Huron
Lake Ontario
Lake Erie

ELECTRICAL POWER LINES AND GENERATING STATIONS

POWER LINES

GENERATING STATIONS
• Hydro
• Fossil Fuel
• Nuclear

Only stations with a total capacity exceeding 100 MW are shown

Thunder Bay
Duluth
Sault Ste. Marie
Sudbury
North Bay
TORONTO
Rochester
Syracuse
Hamilton
Buffalo
Milwaukee
Grand Rapids
Flint
London
Lansing
DETROIT
CHICAGO
Toledo
Cleveland
Fort Wayne

Lake Superior
Lake Michigan
Lake Huron
Lake Ontario
Lake Erie

Levels, Diversions And Consumptive Use Studies

The responsibilities of the International Joint Commission (IJC) for levels and flows of the Great Lakes are separate from its responsibilities for water quality. Water quality objectives are set by the Great Lakes Water Quality Agreement, but decisions about levels and flows are made to comply with the terms of the 1909 Boundary Waters Treaty.

Only limited controls of levels and flows are possible and only for Lake Superior and Lake Ontario. The flows are controlled by locks and dams on the St. Marys River, at Niagara Falls and in the St. Lawrence. Special boards of experts advise the IJC about meeting the terms of the treaty. Members of the binational control boards are equally divided between government agencies in both countries. Until 1973, the IJC managed levels and flows for navigation and hydropower production purposes. Since then, the IJC has tried to balance these interests with prevention of shore erosion.

The IJC has carried out several special studies on levels issues in response to references, or requests, from the governments. In 1964, when water levels were very low, the governments asked the IJC whether it would be feasible to maintain the waters of all the Great Lakes, including Michigan and Huron, at a more constant level. After a 9-year study, in 1973, when water levels were very high, the IJC advised the governments that the high costs of an engineering system for further regulation of Michigan and Huron could not be justified by the benefits. The same conclusion was reached for further regulation of Lake Erie in 1983.

Two human activities, diversion and consumptive use, have potential for affecting lake levels, although they have had relatively little impact to date. Diversion refers to transfer of water from one watershed to another. Consumptive use refers to water that is withdrawn for use and not returned. Most consumptive use in the Great Lakes is caused by evaporation from power plant cooling systems.

At present, water is diverted into the Great Lakes system from the Hudson Bay watershed through Long Lac and Lake Ogoki, and diverted out of the Great Lakes and into the Mississippi watershed at Chicago. These diversions are almost equally balanced and have had little long-term effect on levels of the lakes.

In 1982, the IJC reported on a study of the effects of existing diversions into and out of the Great Lakes system and on consumptive uses. Until this study, consumptive use had not been considered significant for the Great Lakes because the volume of water in the system is so large. The study concluded that climate and weather changes affect levels of the lakes far more than existing human-made diversions. However, the report concluded that if consumptive uses of water continue to increase at historical rates, outflows through the St. Lawrence River could be reduced by as much as 8 percent by around the year 2030.

As illustrated by the hydrograph shown in Chapter two, lake levels vary from year to year and can be expected to continue to do so. Following the period of high lake levels in the 1980s, the IJC conducted another study of levels and the feasibility of modifying them through various means. In 1993, the study concluded that the costs of major engineering works to further regulate the levels and flows of the Great Lakes and St. Lawrence River would exceed the benefits provided and would have negative environmental impacts. Instead, it recommended comprehensive and coordinated land-use and shoreline management programs throughout the basin that would help reduce vulnerability to flood and erosion damages.

Great Lakes Factsheet No. 3A — Water Withdrawals

		Superior	Michigan	Huron	Erie	Ontario	TOTALS
Municipal							
Canada	*	40		120	190	660	1,010
	**	36		107	170	589	902
U.S.	*	70	2,940	310	2,820	380	6,520
	**	62	2,262	277	2,515	339	5,455
Total	*	110	2,940	430	3,010	1,040	7,530
	**	98	2,622	384	2,685	927	6,716
Manufacturing							
Canada	*	860		1,360	1,900	2,760	6,880
	**	767		1,213	1,694	2,462	6,136
U.S.	*	410	9,650	1,060	9,110	530	20,760
	**	366	8,608	945	8,126	473	18,518
Total	*	1,270	9,650	2,420	11,010	3,290	27,640
	**	1,133	8,608	2,158	9,820	2,935	24,652
Power Production							
Canada	*	70		2,870	1,160	8,370	12,470
	**	62		2,560	1,035	7,466	11,123
U.S.	*	760	13,600	2,570	13,180	6,520	36,360
	**	678	12,131	2,292	11,757	5,816	32,674
Total	*	830	13,600	5,440	14,340	14,890	49,100
	**	740	12,131	4,852	12,791	13,282	43,796
GRAND TOTALS							
	*	2,210	26,190	8,290	28,360	19,220	84,270
	**	1,971	23,361	7,394	25,296	17,144	75,166

* Cubic feet per second
** Millions of cubic metres per year

Source: BULLETINS E-1866-70, Sea Grant College Program, Cooperative Extension Service, Michigan State University, E. Lansing, Michigan, 1985.

Great Lakes Factsheet No. 3B — Water Consumed

		Superior	Michigan	Huron	Erie	Ontario	TOTALS
Municipal							
Canada	*	10		20	30	100	160
	**	9		18	27	89	143
U.S.	*	10	190	170	280	70	720
	**	9	169	152	257	62	649
Total	*	20	190	190	210	170	780
	**	18	169	170	189	152	698
Manufacturing							
Canada	*	20		70	80	100	270
	**	18		62	71	89	240
U.S.	*	60	880	30	1,500	40	2,510
	**	53	785	27	1,338	36	2,239
Total	*	80	880	100	1,580	140	2,780
	**	71	785	89	1,409	125	2,479
Power Production							
Canada	*	0		20	10	60	90
	**	0		18	9	54	81
U.S.	*	10	240	50	190	120	610
	**	9	214	45	169	108	545
Total	*	10	240	70	200	180	700
	**	9	214	62	178	174	673
GRAND TOTALS							
	*	110	1,310	360	1,990	490	4,260
	**	98	1,168	321	1,776	451	3,814

* Cubic feet per second
** Millions of cubic metres per year

Source: BULLETINS E-1866-70, Sea Grant College Program, Cooperative Extension Service, Michigan State University, E. Lansing, Michigan, 1985.

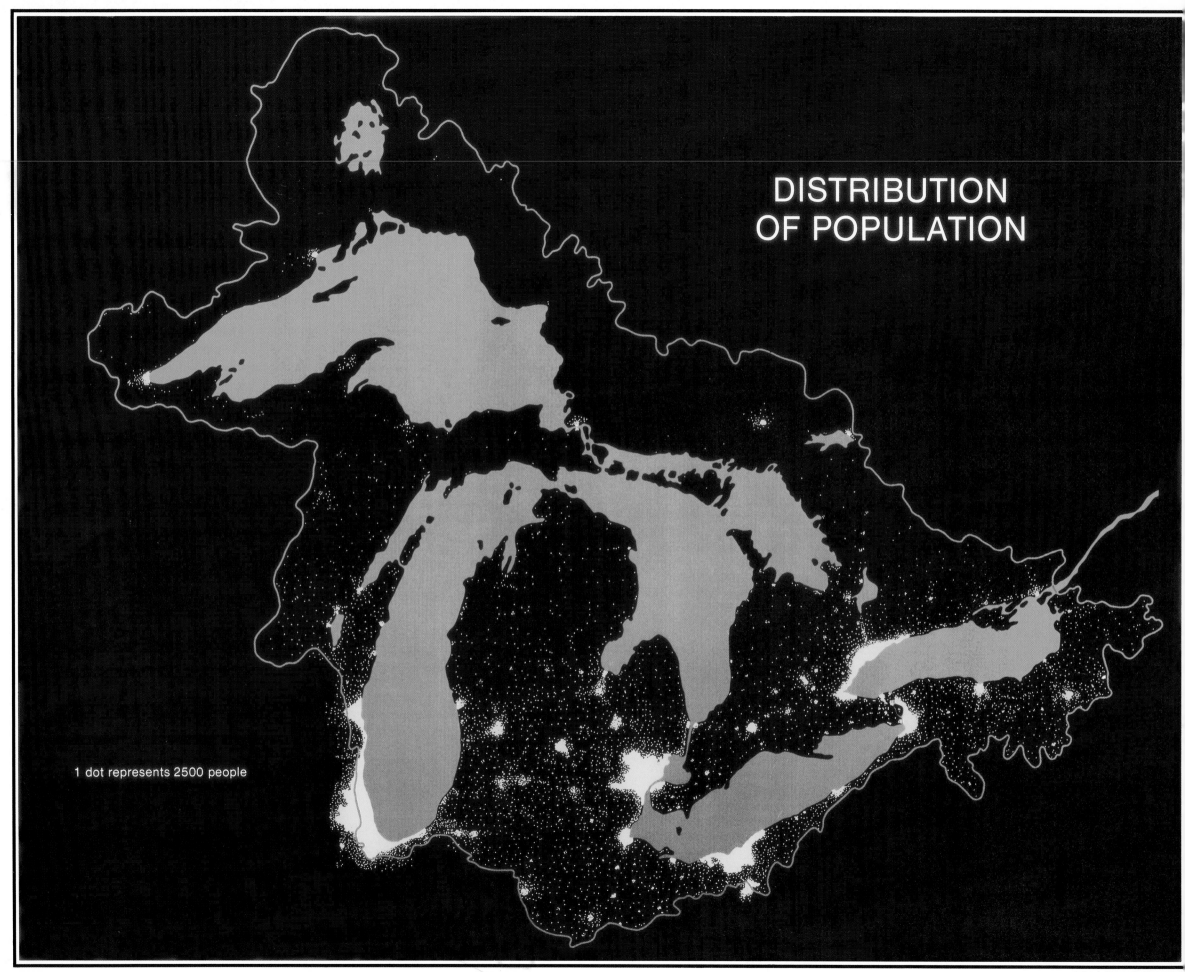

DISTRIBUTION
OF POPULATION

1 dot represents 2500 people

THE GREAT LAKES
Today
– CONCERNS

Wilderness is the raw material out of which man has hammered the artifact called civilization ... No living man will see again the virgin pineries of the Lake states, or the flatwoods of the coastal plain, or the giant hardwoods ...
– Aldo Leopold

While parts of the Great Lakes ecosystem have been changed to better suit the needs of humans, the unexpected consequences of many of the changes have only recently become apparent. Since about 1960, there has been an awakening to the magnitude of these changes and the harsher implications of some human activities. The largest categories of impact are pollution, habitat loss and exotic species.

Deterioration in water quality and habitat began with modern settlement. At first the impact was localized. Agricultural development, forestry and urbanization caused streams and shoreline marshes to silt up and harbor areas to become septic. Domestic and industrial waste discharges, oil and chemical spills and the effects of mining left some parts of the waterways unfit for water supply and recreation. Waste-treatment solutions were adopted to treat biological pollutants that threatened the immediate health of populations. In some jurisdictions, regulations were passed to prevent capricious dumping in the waterways. Eventually, however, it took a major threat to the whole Great Lakes basin to awaken authorities to the fact that the entire Great Lakes ecosystem was being damaged.

PATHOGENS

Historically, the primary reason for water pollution control was prevention of waterborne disease. Municipalities began treating drinking water by adding chlorine, as a disinfectant. This proved to be a simple solution to a very serious public health problem, throughout the water distribution system. Chlorine is still used because it is able to kill pathogens throughout the distribution system.

Humans can acquire bacterial, viral and parasitic diseases through direct body contact with contaminated water as well as by drinking the water. Preventing disease

Modern, large-scale agriculture, with its reliance on synthetic fertilizers and pesticides, is one of the main nonpoint sources of pollution to the Great Lakes.

transmission of this kind usually means closing affected beaches during the summer when the water is warm and when bacteria from human and animal feces reach higher concentrations. This is usually attributed to the common practice of combining storm and sanitary sewers in urban areas. Although this practice has been discontinued, existing combined sewers contribute to contamination problems during periods of high rainfall and urban runoff. At these times, sewage collection and treatment systems cannot

handle the large volumes of combined storm and sanitary flow. The result is that untreated sewage, diluted by urban runoff, is discharged directly into waterways.

Remedial action can be very costly if the preferred solution is replacement of the combined sewers in urban areas with separate storm and sanitary sewers. However, alternative techniques such as combined sewer overflow retention for later treatment can be used, greatly reducing the problem at lower costs than sewer separation. Beach closures have become more infrequent with improved treatment of sewage effluent.

EUTROPHICATION AND OXYGEN DEPLETION

Lakes can be characterized by their biological productivity, that is, the amount of living material supported within them, primarily in the form of algae. The least productive lakes are called 'oligotrophic'; those with intermediate productivity are 'mesotrophic'; and the most productive are 'eutrophic'. The variables that determine productivity are temperature, light, depth and volume, and the amount of nutrients received from the environment.

Except in shallow bays and shoreline marshes, the Great Lakes were 'oligotrophic' before European settlement and industrialization. Their size, depth and the climate kept them continuously cool and clear. The lakes received small amounts of fertilizers such as

phosphorus and nitrogen from decomposing organic material in runoff from forested lands. Small amounts of nitrogen and phosphorus also came from the atmosphere.

These conditions have changed. Temperatures of many tributaries have been increased by removal of vegetative shade cover and some by thermal pollution. But, more importantly, the amount of nutrients and organic material entering the lakes has increased with intensified urbanization and agriculture. Nutrient loading increased with the advent of phosphate detergents and inorganic fertilizers. Although controlled in most jurisdictions bordering the Great Lakes, phosphates in detergents continue to be a problem where they are not regulated.

Increased nutrients in the lakes stimulate the growth of green plants, including algae. The amount of plant growth increases rapidly in the same way that applying lawn fertilizers (nitrogen, phosphorus and potassium) results in rapid, green growth. In the aquatic system the increased plant life eventually dies, settles to the bottom and decomposes. During decomposition, the organisms that break down the plants use up oxygen dissolved in the water near the bottom. With more growth there is more material to be decomposed, and more consumption of oxygen. Under normal conditions, when nutrient loadings are low, dissolved oxygen levels are maintained by the diffusion of oxygen into water, mixing by currents and wave action, and by the oxygen production of photosynthesizing plants.

Depletion of oxygen through decomposition of organic material is known as biochemical oxygen demand (BOD), which is generated from two different sources. In tributaries and harbors it is often caused by materials contained in the discharges from treatment plants. The other principal source is decaying algae. In large embayments and open lake areas such as the central basin of Lake Erie, algal BOD is the primary problem.

As the BOD load increases and as oxygen levels drop, certain species of fish can be killed and pollution-tolerant species that require less oxygen, such as sludge worms and carp, replace the original species. Changes in species of algae, bottom-dwelling organisms (or benthos) and fish are therefore biological indicators of oxygen depletion.

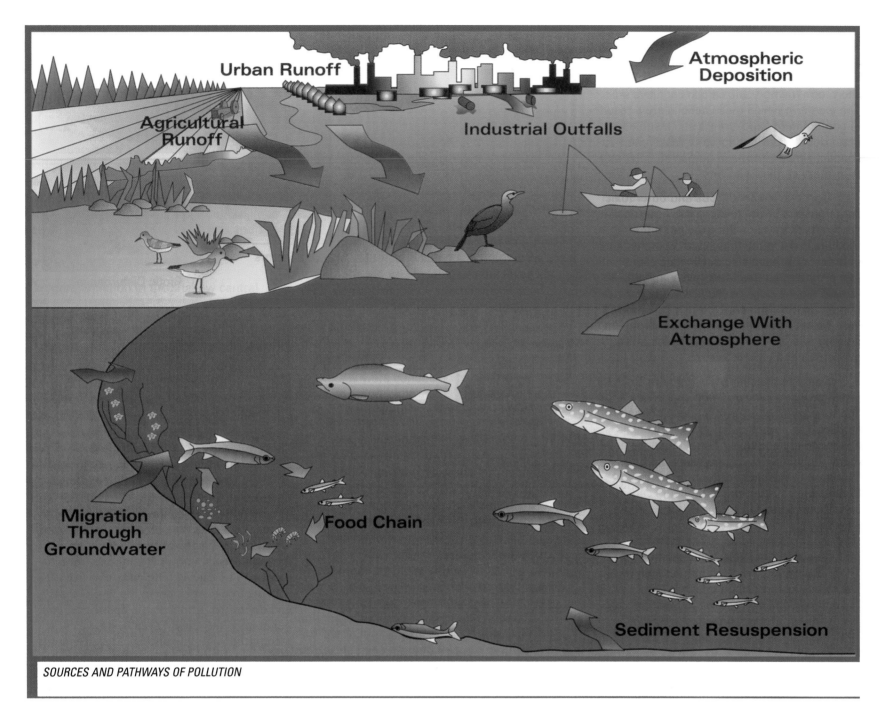

Urban Runoff

Atmospheric Deposition

Agricultural Runoff

Industrial Outfalls

Exchange With Atmosphere

Migration Through Groundwater

Food Chain

Sediment Resuspension

SOURCES AND PATHWAYS OF POLLUTION

Groundwater movement is another pathway for pollutants. As water slowly passes through the ground it can pick up dissolved materials that have been buried or soaked into the ground. Contamination of groundwater tends to be localized near badly contaminated sites, but it can also be wide-spread if the pollutant was used as a pesticide. Because treatment of groundwater is very difficult and expensive, prevention is clearly the best approach.

Surface runoff is the pathway for a wide variety of substances that enter the lakes. Nutrients, pesticides and soils are released by agricultural activities. In urban areas, street runoff includes automobile-related substances such as salt, sand, asbestos, cadmium, lead, oils and greases. Surface runoff also includes a wide number of materials deposited with precipitation, which may include particulates, bacteria, nutrients and toxic substances.

LOADINGS TO A CLOSED SYSTEM

In considering pathways of pollution, it is important to recognize that in the case of the Great Lakes, unlike rivers that run to the oceans, pathways end in the lakes. Regardless of whether pollutants are diluted by large stream flows or temporarily stored on sediment particles on stream bottoms, they will eventually reach the lakes and add to the total burden.

Because the lakes respond to total quantities of persistent substances as well as localized concentrations, it is important to understand the total loading of pollutants to each lake from all pathways. This was first recognized for phosphorus, as reflected in the Great Lakes Water Quality Agreement.

As laboratory capability for analysis has improved together with the understanding of how persistent toxic substances cycle in the ecosystem, total loadings are becoming known. This knowledge, together with bioaccumulation factors, can translate loadings into predictable levels in biota. These developments hold the promise that the Lakewide Management Plans called for in the Agreement can provide the 'schedule of load

Transport of substances such as PCBs is complicated by the fact that they tend not to stay dissolved in water and thus volatilize back into the atmosphere or become attached to particles. As a result, large quantities of PCBs volatilize out of the lakes, as well as being deposited into them from the vast reservoir of synthetic organic chemicals moving about in regional and global air masses.

Sediments that were contaminated before pollutant discharges were regulated

are another source of pollution. Such in-place pollutants are a problem in most urban-industrial areas. Release of pollutants from sediments is believed to be occurring in connecting channels such as the Niagara, St. Clair and St. Marys Rivers, in harbors such as Hamilton, Toronto and the Grand Calumet, and in tributaries such as the Buffalo, Ashtabula and Black Rivers. Even where it is possible to remove highly contaminated sediments from harbors, removal can cause

problems when sediments are placed in landfills that may later leak and contaminate wetlands and groundwater. Dredging for navigation can also present problems of disposal of dredge spoils. Disposal of highly polluted sediments in the open lakes has been prohibited since the 1960s. In both the U.S. and Canada, research and demonstration projects are being conducted to find effective ways to isolate, remove and destroy contaminated sediments.

reductions of Critical Pollutants that would result in meeting Agreement Objectives'.

CONTROL OF POLLUTANTS

As major progress has been made in control of industrial and municipal discharges to waterways, the importance of other sources has become better understood.

Direct discharges to waterways are known as point sources. Because such sources have specific owners and can be easily sampled, regulatory programs have resulted in a high degree of control. Nonpoint sources include urban and agricultural runoff, airborne deposition of pollutants from automobiles and commercial activities, and contaminated sediments and contaminated groundwater. Control of nonpoint sources is made difficult by their diffuse nature, episodic release and lack of institutional arrangements to support their control.

Because of the myriad of widespread contributors, nonpoint sources are far less suited to regulatory control. As a consequence, public education, pollution prevention and voluntary actions are very important. The importance of pollution prevention is gaining increasing recognition both as an effective means of dealing with nonpoint pollution and in dealing with pollutants from point sources that continue to cause problems even after state-of-the-art treatment has been applied. Pollution prevention focuses on eliminating pollutants before they are produced. This includes changing production processes and feedstocks, and choice of environmentally benign products by consumers.

One preventive approach has been to ban the production/extraction and use of certain individual chemicals and metals and to prevent the direct discharge of others into waterways. The production and use of DDT were banned after it was shown that the pesticide thinned the shells of bird eggs, causing reproductive failures. The levels of DDT in the environment began to decline immediately following regulation. In the case of PCBs, production has been banned but their use is still being phased out.

Bioaccumulation And Biomagnification

The nutrients necessary for plant growth (e.g., nitrogen and phosphorus) are found at very low concentrations in most natural waters. In order to obtain sufficient quantities for growth, phytoplankton must collect these chemical elements from a relatively large volume of water.

In the process of collecting nutrients, they also collect certain human-made chemicals, such as some persistent pesticides. These may be present in the water at concentrations so low that they cannot be measured even by very sensitive instruments. The chemicals, however, biologically accumulate (bioaccumulate) in the organism and become concentrated at levels that are much higher in the living cells than in the open water. This is especially true for persistent chemicals – substances that do not break down readily in the environment – like DDT and PCBs that are stored in fatty tissues.

The small fish and zooplankton eat vast quantities of phytoplankton. In doing so, any toxic chemicals accumulated by the phytoplankton are further concentrated in the bodies of the animals that eat them. This is repeated at each step in the food chain. This process of increasing concentration through the food chain is known as biomagnification.

The top predators at the end of a long food chain, such as lake trout, large salmon and fish-eating gulls, may accumulate concentrations of a toxic chemical high enough to cause serious deformities or death even though the concentration of the chemical in the open water is extremely low. The concentration of some chemicals in the fatty tissues of top predators can be millions of times higher than the concentration in the open water.

The eggs of aquatic birds often have some of the highest concentrations of toxic chemicals, because they are at the end of a long aquatic food chain, and because egg yolk is rich in fatty material. Thus, the first harmful effects of a toxic chemical in a lake often appear as dead or malformed chicks. Scientists monitor colonies of gulls and other water birds because these effects can serve as early warning signs of a growing toxic chemical problem. They also collect gull eggs for chemical analysis because toxic chemicals will be detectable in them long before they reach measurable levels in the open water.

Research of this kind is important to humans as well, because they are consumers in the Great Lakes food chain. Humans are at the top of many food chains, but do not receive as high an exposure as, for example, herring gulls. This is because humans have a varied diet that consists of items from all levels of the food chain, whereas the herring gull depends upon fish as its sole food source. Nevertheless, the concerns about long-term effects of low-level exposures in humans, as well as impacts on people who do eat a lot of contaminated fish and wildlife, highlight the importance of taking heed of the well-documented adverse effects already seen in the ecosystem.

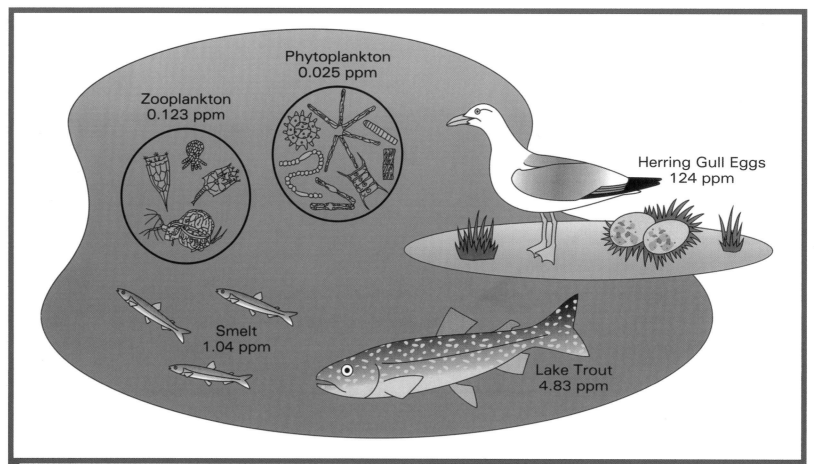

PERSISTENT ORGANIC CHEMICALS such as PCBs bioaccumulate. This diagram shows the degree of concentration in each level of the Great Lakes aquatic food chain for PCBs (in parts per million, ppm). The highest levels are reached in the eggs of fish-eating birds such as herring gulls.

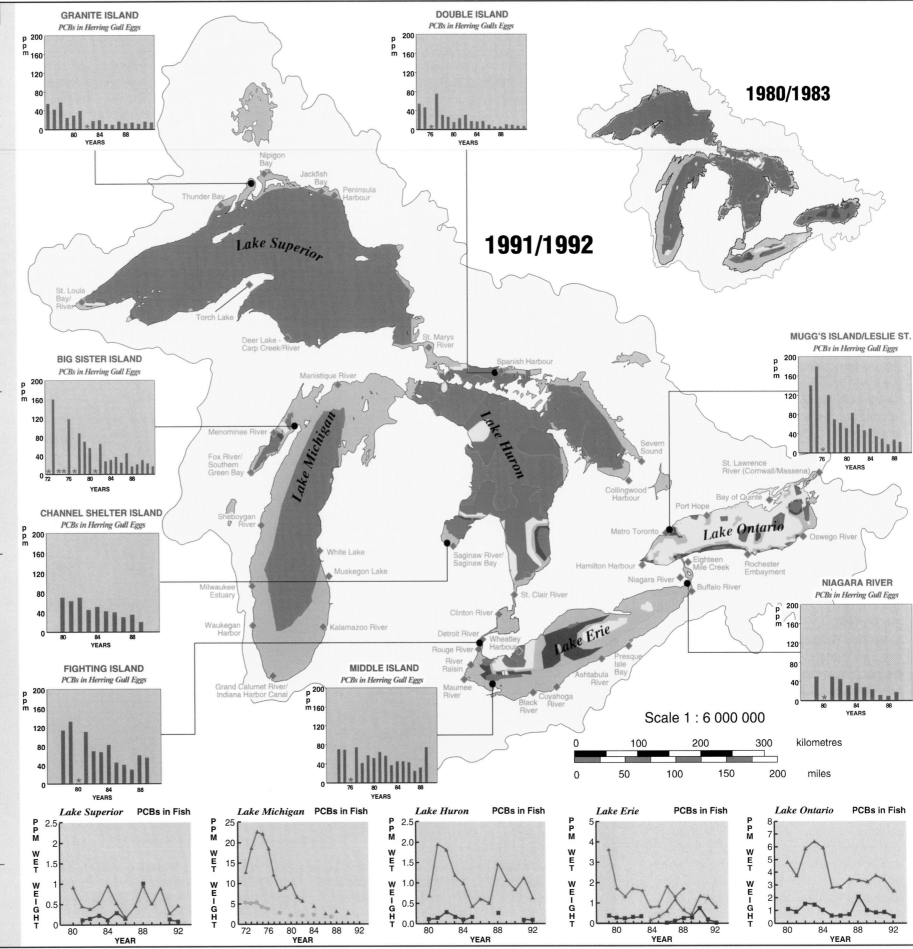

STATE OF THE LAKES

PHOSPHORUS CONCENTRATIONS

Main map represents total phosphorus concentrations for 1991/1992

Insert map represents total phosphorus concentrations for 1980/1983

<0.005 mg/L	0.012 - 0.015
0.005 - 0.0069	>0.015 mg/L
0.007 - 0.0099	not generated by computer simulation
0.010 - 0.0119	

This map of phosphorus concentrations is a generalization produced by computer analysis. It is intended to illustrate the change in general conditions between two time periods and should not be assumed to be accurate for specific sites.

PCBs IN GULL EGGS

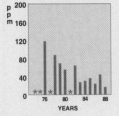

PCBs in Herring Gull Eggs

Trends in average annual concentrations of PCBs in herring gull eggs at eight colonies on the Great Lakes.

★ - indicates no data

PCBs IN FISH

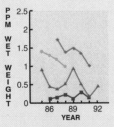

Lake Superior - Mean concentrations of PCBs (ppm wet weight +/- standard error) in whole rainbow smelt and lake trout (age 4). Data were not available in consecutive years

Lake Michigan - Mean concentrations of PCBs (ppm wet weight) in whole bloater and lake trout (620-640 mm mean length). Data were not available in consecutive years.

- Lake Trout
- Rainbow Smelt
- Bloater
- Walleye

Lake Huron - Mean concentrations of PCBs in whole rainbow smelt and lake trout (age 4). Data were not available in consecutive years.

Lake Erie - Mean concentrations of PCBs (ppm wet weight +/- standard error) in whole rainbow smelt and walleye.

Lake Ontario - Mean concentrations of PCBs (ppm wet weight +/- standard error) in whole rainbow smelt and lake trout (age 4).

AREAS OF CONCERN

The diamond symbol marks areas of concern. There are 43 Areas of Concern in the Great Lakes basin. ◆

Scale 1 : 6 000 000

Geomatics International Cartography

Th...
to mana...
loped o...
and the...
standing...
resulted...
in the b...
monitor...
protecti...
of both...
come th...
levels. E...
involver...
well as i...
zations,...
and ofte...
the basi...

Or...
a separa...
strated ...
and wat...
the nee...
ecosyste...
use of v...
States a...
instituti...

Th...
due to i...
were co...
solution...
minatior...
mouths...

Comn...
proce...
healtl...
proje...
susta...
set by...
secto...

Peopl...
Areas...
Resid...
ask q...
addre...

Peopl...
swee...
recyc...
also p...

includes the ca...
intact, to self-re...
or external stre...
increasing com...

Overall, v...
improving due...
made in contro...
wastes from m...
under environn...
1960s. Even so,...
impairment of...
fishing, swimm...
environmental...

Serious p...
the basin in loc...
of Concern'. Ar...
geographic are...
water or biota i...
environmental...
extent that use...
to exist. The pu...
Concern is to e...
partnerships w...
bilitate these ac...
and to restore 1...
areas, existing...
expected to be...
quality to accer...
are needed. Ju...
Remedial Actio...
rehabilitation a...
Area of Concer...
has been clean...

Most IJC ...
the mouths of 1...
industries are l...
are along the c...
the lakes. Pollu...
these areas bec...
tion of contami...
point and nonp...
upstream sourc...
of Concern hav...

Over the l...
the problems a...
has changed. F...
made in restori...
reducing some...
lead and mercu...
the problem of...

HABITAT AND BIODIVERSITY

Habitat within the Great Lakes basin has been significantly altered following the arrival of European settlers, especially during the last 150 years. Nearly all of the existing forests have been cut at least once and the forest and prairie soils suited to agriculture have been plowed or intensively grazed. This, together with construction of dams and urbanization, has created vast changes in the plant and animal populations. Streams have been changed not only by direct physical disturbance, but by sedimentation and changes in runoff rates due to changing land use, and by increases in temperature caused by removal of shading vegetation.

Wetlands are a key category of habitat within the basin because of their importance to the aquatic plant and animal communities. Many natural wetlands have been filled in or drained for agriculture, urban uses, shoreline development, recreation and resource extraction (peat mining). Losses have been particularly high in the southern portions of the basin. It is estimated, for example, that between 70 and 80 percent of the original wetlands of Southern Ontario have been lost since European settlement, and losses in the U.S. portion of the basin range from 42 percent in Minnesota to 92 percent in Ohio. Unfortunately, some governments continue to encourage this practice through drainage subsidies to farmers. The loss of these lands poses special problems for hydrological processes and water quality because of the natural storage and cleansing functions of wetlands. Moreover, the loss makes difficult the preservation and protection of certain wildlife species that require wetlands for part or all of their life cycle.

Biodiversity refers to both the number of species and the genetic diversity within populations of each species. Some species have become extinct as a result of changes within the Great Lakes basin and many others are being threatened with extinction or loss of important genetic diversity. Recovery of some highly visible species such as eagles and cormorants has been dramatic, but other less known species remain in danger.

The loss of genetic diversity or variability within a species is a less well understood problem. An example is the loss of genetic stocks of fish that instinctively spawn or feed in certain areas or under certain conditions. This is thought to be a factor in the lack of recovery of some species such as lake trout, which are apparently not able to sustain naturally reproducing populations except in Lake Superior. Even in Lake Superior all of the genetic strains of lake trout that once spawned in tributaries have been lost. Lack of diversity within a species can also increase the vulnerability of the population to catastrophic loss caused by disease or a major change in environmental conditions.

As many forms of pollution have been controlled and reduced, the importance of habitat is being recognized as critically important to the health of the Great Lakes ecosystem. As the physical, chemical and biological interactions of the ecosystem are becoming better understood, it has become apparent that no one component can be viewed in isolation. To protect any living component, its habitat and place within the system must be protected.

EXOTIC SPECIES

An equally important cause of change has been the introduction of exotic, i.e., non-native, species of plants and animals. In the lakes, sea lamprey, carp, smelt, alewife, Pacific salmon and zebra mussels, to name just a few, have had highly visible impacts. The effects of hundreds of other invading organisms are less obvious, but can be profound. On land, invading plants such as purple loosestrife and European buckthorn continue to displace native species. In some areas, major changes in terrestrial plant communities have been caused by suppression of fire. All of these disturbances have resulted in changes in aquatic and terrestrial habitat, causing further changes in plant and animal populations. The collective result has been the disruption of the complex communities of plants and animals that had evolved during thousands of years of presettlement conditions. Destruction of these complex communities by changes in land use or by invasion by exotic species has resulted in loss of biodiversity.

SUSTAINABLE DEVELOPMENT

Pollution prevention, protecting and restoring habitat, protecting biodiversity, understanding the ecosystem and cleaning up old pollution problems are all a part of sustainable development. The term 'sustainable development' first gained visibility in the report of the World Commission on Environment and Development, commonly known as the Bruntland Commission. The report, entitled 'Our Common Future', defined the concept generally as the process of change in which the exploitation of resources, the direction of investments, the orientation of technological development and institutional change are made consistent with future as well as present needs. If the Parties to the Great Lakes Water Quality Agreement are to fulfill its purpose 'to restore and maintain the chemical, physical and biological integrity of the waters of the Great Lakes Basin Ecosystem' it is clear that attaining sustainable development within both countries is essential.

A major test of whether sustainable development has been achieved will be whether this integrity has been restored or maintained. The concept of integrity of an ecosystem recognizes that ecosystems contain mechanisms that create both stability and resiliency within them. Integrity

This shopping cart was left in zebra mussel-infested waters for a few months. The mussels have colonized every available surface on the cart.

Success in reducing phosphorus loadings under the Great Lakes Water Quality Agreement has provided a model to the world in binational resource management. The use of the mass balance approach for phosphorus set the stage for the much more difficult task of controlling toxic contamination. Further progress in cleaning up pollution from the past and preventing future degradation depends on fully applying an ecosystem approach to management.

THE GREAT LAKES WATER QUALITY AGREEMENT – 1987

In 1987, the Agreement was revised to strengthen management provisions, call for development of ecosystem objectives and indicators, and address nonpoint sources of pollution, contaminated sediment airborne toxic substances and pollution from contaminated groundwater. New management approaches included development of Remedial Action Plans (RAPs) for geographic Areas of Concern and Lakewide Management Plans (LAMPs) for Critical Pollutants.

The ecosystem approach was strengthened by calling for development of ecosystem objectives and indicators, and by focusing RAPs and LAMPs on elimination of impairments of beneficial uses. The uses include various aspects of human and aquatic community health and specifically include habitat. By clearly focusing management activities on endpoints in the living system, additional meaning is given to the goal of restoring and maintaining the integrity of the Great Lakes basin ecosystem.

The agreement to prepare Lakewide Management Plans includes a commitment to develop a schedule of reductions in loads of critical pollutants entering the lakes in order to meet water quality objectives and restore beneficial uses. Thus the mass balance concept developed for phosphorus is being applied to control of toxic substances into the Great Lakes. Although total elimination of toxic substances from the Great Lakes basin

is the goal, the mass balance approach can be used to set priorities and direct pollution control efforts.

AN ECOSYSTEM APPROACH TO MANAGEMENT

The adoption of an ecosystem approach to management is the result of growing understanding of the many interrelated and interdependent factors that govern the ecological health of the Great Lakes. An ecosystem approach does not depend on any one program or course of action. Rather it assumes a more comprehensive and interdisciplinary attitude that leads to wide interpretation of its practical meaning. Certain basic characteristics, however, mark the ecosystem approach.

First, it takes a broad, systemic view of the interaction among physical, chemical and biological components in the Great Lakes basin. The interdependence of the life in the lakes and the chemical/physical characteristics of the water is reflected in the use of biological indicators to monitor water quality and changes in the aquatic ecosystem. Examples include the use of herring gull eggs as an indicator of toxic pollutants, algal blooms as an indicator of accelerated eutrophication and changes in species composition of aquatic communities as an indicator of habitat destruction. Biomonitoring for chronic toxicity can use zooplankton and phytoplankton to measure the effects of long-term exposure to low levels of a toxic chemical on growth and reproduction.

Second, the ecosystem approach is geographically comprehensive, covering the entire system including land, air and water. New emphasis on the importance of atmospheric inputs of pollutants and the effects of land uses on water quality are evidence of the broad scope of management planning required in an ecosystem approach.

Finally, the ecosystem approach includes humans as a major factor in the well-being of the system. This suggests recognition of social, economic, technical and political variables that affect how humans use natural resources. Human culture, changing lifestyles and attitudes must be considered in an ecosystem approach because of their effects on the integrity of the ecosystem.

The ecosystem approach is a departure from an earlier focus on localized pollution, management of separate components of the ecosystem in isolation and planning that neglects the profound influences of land uses on water quality. It is a framework for decision making that compels managers and planners to cooperate in devising integrated strategies of research and action to restore and protect the integrity of the Great Lakes ecosystem for the future. The evolution of management programs toward a full ecosystem approach is still in its early stages, but progress is being made.

Long Point on Lake Erie is an example of a high-quality ecosystem rich in biodiversity.

Earlier chapters have described the resources of the Great Lakes, how humans have used and benefited from them, and the physical, biological and chemical impacts of human activity. As the story of the Great Lakes unfolds, the importance of protecting and preserving the lakes is highlighted. The previous chapter mapped the development of an involved, broad-based 'community' of Great Lakes concern. Citizens from all sectors of society are discovering their own personal connection to the Great Lakes. As a result, they are becoming increasingly involved in actions to protect and preserve this vital ecosystem.

CHAPTER SIX

NEW DIRECTIONS
for the
GREAT LAKES COMMUNITY

and habitats of the Great Lakes basin is needed to support protection and rehabilitation of the biodiversity of the ecosystem and to strengthen management of natural resources. Wetlands, forests, shorelines and other environmentally sensitive areas will have to be more strictly protected and, in some cases, rehabilitated and expanded.

As health protection measures are taken and environmental cleanup continues, rehabilitation of degraded areas and prevention of further damage are being recognized as the best way to promote good health, and protect and preserve the living resources and habitats of the Great Lakes.

COOPERATION

The surge of public involvement in management of the Great Lakes reflects the change in attitudes toward the lakes over the years. The belief in earlier times that the effects of pollution were necessary results of prosperity and progress has given way to the philosophy that the Great Lakes ecosystem must be managed responsibly and treated respectfully.

Cooperation on many fronts highlights the commitment of the people of the United States and Canada to prevent further degradation and to protect the future of the Great Lakes. This commitment has been reflected through the Great Lakes Water Quality Agreement, national programs for environmental protection and the involvement of governments, non-government agencies and groups, researchers, industries, communities and individuals.

The public's direct actions have influenced both governments and industry. Together, citizens from both sides of the border have provided the impetus for governments to cooperate and adopt more creative and effective management solutions to Great Lakes problems. The concept of an ecosystem approach to management has become reality from the experiences of this broad-based Great Lakes community.

RESEARCH

Research conducted in universities and government agencies is contributing a substantial body of theory and information for practical management programs, and a better understanding of the ecosystem and its properties. Research continues to look for solutions to existing and emerging problems.

The refinement of mass balance and biomonitoring techniques is an ongoing task. There is still an urgent need to understand how toxic substances move through the Great Lakes ecosystem on land, in the air, by water and through the food web. More information is needed about less obvious, nonpoint pollution sources to the Great Lakes, such as land runoff, long-range transport of contaminants in the atmosphere into the Great Lakes basin, movement of chemicals in groundwater and secondary pollution that may occur when substances combine chemically in air or water.

Research is required to answer human health questions, to promote improved human health and to prevent disease. Indicators of human and ecosystem health must be developed and supported by ecosystem monitoring. The extent to which the ecosystem is affected by the hormone-like effects of persistent chlorinated substances must be determined.

THE FUTURE OF THE GREAT LAKES

The story of the Great Lakes does not end here. Although progress has been steady and the ecosystem has shown signs of recovery, pollution will continue to be a major concern in the years to come. A broader scope of regulation of toxic chemicals may be necessary as research and monitoring reveal practices that are harmful. More stringent controls of waste disposal are already being applied in many locations. Agricultural practices are being examined because of the far-reaching effects of pesticides and fertilizers. In addition to pollution problems, better understanding of the living resources

PEOPLE IN THE ECOSYSTEM

As people living around the lakes make the connection between themselves and the Great Lakes, they will become increasingly involved in positive actions. People are indeed reclaiming, cleaning up and restoring their watersheds, local shorelines, parks and green space. Through careful management of technology and economic development, people can live within the ecosystem without causing injury. In return, the lakes and the lands surrounding them will continue to contribute to the quality of life for the people of the region and all living things in the Great Lakes ecosystem and beyond.

Glossary

ALGA (pl. ALGAE) - Simple one-celled or many-celled micro-organisms capable of carrying on photosynthesis in aquatic ecosystems.

ANOXIA - The absence of oxygen necessary for sustaining most life. In aquatic ecosystems, this refers to the absence of dissolved oxygen in water.

AREA OF CONCERN - An area recognized by the International Joint Commission where 1 or more of 14 beneficial uses are impaired or where objectives of the Great Lakes Water Quality Agreement or local environmental standards are not being achieved.

ATMOSPHERIC DEPOSITION - Pollution from the atmosphere associated with dry deposition in the form of dust, wet deposition in the form of rain and snow, or as a result of vapor exchanges.

BIOCHEMICAL OXYGEN DEMAND - The amount of dissolved oxygen required for the bacterial decomposition of organic waste in water.

BIOMAGNIFICATION - A cumulative increase in the concentration of a persistent substance in successively higher trophic levels of the food chain (i.e., from algae to zooplankton to fish to birds).

BIOMASS - Total dry weight of all living organisms in a given area.

BIOMONITORING - The use of organisms to test the acute toxicity of substances in effluent discharges as well as the chronic toxicity of low-level pollutants in the ambient aquatic environment.

CARCINOGEN - Cancer-causing chemicals, substances or radiation.

CONSUMPTIVE USE - Permanent removal of water from a water body. Consumptive use may be due to evaporation or incorporation of water into a manufactured product.

DDT - Dichloro-diphenyl-trichloroethane - a widely used, very persistent pesticide in the chlorinated hydrocarbon group, now banned from production and use in many countries.

DISSOLVED OXYGEN - The amount of oxygen dissolved in water. See ANOXIA and BIOCHEMICAL OXYGEN DEMAND.

DIVERSION - Transfer of water from one watershed to another.

DRAINAGE BASIN - A waterbody and the land area drained by it.

ECOSYSTEM - The interacting complex of living organisms and their non-living environment.

EFFLUENT - Waste waters discharged from industrial or municipal sewage treatment plants.

EPILIMNION - The warm, upper layer of water that occurs in a lake during summer stratification.

EROSION - The wearing away and transportation of soils, rocks and dissolved minerals from the land surface or along shorelines by rainfall, running water, or wave and current action.

EUTROPHICATION - The process of fertilization that causes high productivity and biomass in an aquatic ecosystem. Eutrophication can be a natural process or it can be a cultural process accelerated by an increase of nutrient loading to a lake by human activity.

EXOTIC SPECIES - Species that are not native to the Great Lakes and have been intentionally introduced or have inadvertently infiltrated the system.

FOOD WEB - The process by which organisms in higher trophic levels gain energy by consuming organisms at lower trophic levels.

HUMAN HEALTH - The state of complete physical, mental and social well-being and not merely the absence of disease or infirmity (World Health Organization).

HYDROLOGIC CYCLE - The natural cycle of water on earth, including precipitation as rain and snow, runoff from land, storage in lakes, streams, and oceans, and evaporation and transpiration (from plants) into the atmosphere.

HYPOLIMNION - The cold, dense, lower layer of water that occurs in a lake during summer stratification.

LEACHATE - Materials suspended or dissolved in water and other liquids, usually from waste sites, which percolate through soils and rock layers.

MASS BALANCE - An approach to evaluating the source, transport and fate of contaminants entering a water system as well as their effects on water quality.

MESOTROPHIC - See TROPHIC STATUS

MONOCULTURE - Agriculture that is based on a single type of crop.

NONPOINT SOURCE - Source of pollution in which pollutants are discharged over a widespread area or from a number of small inputs rather than from distinct, identifiable sources.

NUTRIENT - A chemical that is an essential raw material for the growth and development of organisms.

OLIGOTROPHIC - See TROPHIC STATUS

PATHOGENS - Disease-causing agents such as bacteria, viruses and parasites.

PCBs - polychlorinated biphenyls - A class of persistent organic chemicals that bioaccumulate.

PHOTOSYNTHESIS - A process occurring in the cells of green plants and some micro-organisms in which solar energy is transformed into stored chemical energy.

PHYTOPLANKTON - Minute, microscopic aquatic plant life (see ALGA).

POINT SOURCE POLLUTION - A source of pollution that is distinct and identifiable, such as an outfall pipe from an industrial plant.

PRODUCTIVITY - The conversion of sunlight and nutrients into plant material through photosynthesis, and the subsequent conversion of this plant material into animal matter.

RESUSPENSION (of sediment) - The remixing of sediment particles and pollutants back into the water by storms, currents, organisms and human activities such as dredging or shipping.

SEICHE - An oscillation in water level from one end of a lake to another due to rapid changes in winds and atmospheric pressure. Most dramatic after an intense but local weather disturbance passes over one end of a large lake.

STRATIFICATION (or LAYERING) - The tendency in deep lakes for distinct layers of water to form as a result of vertical change in temperature and therefore in the density of water. See also EPILIMNION, HYPOLIMNION, THERMOCLINE

THERMOCLINE - A layer of water in deep lakes separating the cool hypolimnion (lower layer) from the warm epilimnion (surface layer).

TOXIC SUBSTANCE - As defined in the Great Lakes Water Quality Agreement, any substance that adversely affects the health or well-being of any living organism.

TROPHIC STATUS - A measure of the biological productivity in a body of water. Aquatic ecosystems are characterized as oligotrophic (low productivity), mesotrophic (medium productivity) or eutrophic (high productivity).

WIND SET-UP - A local rise in water levels caused by winds pushing water to one side of a lake.

ZOOPLANKTON - Minute aquatic animal life.

CONVERSION TABLE
Metric to Imperial Values

1 metre =	3.28 feet
1 kilometre =	0.621 miles
1 kilogram =	2.2 pounds
1 square kilometre =	0.386 square miles
1 cubic kilometre =	0.24 cubic miles
1 litre =	0.264 U.S. gallons
1 cubic metre/second =	35.31 cubic feet/second
1 tonne =	1.1 short tons

References and Suggestions for Further Reading

Allardice, D., and S. Thorp. STATE OF THE LAKES ECOSYSTEM CONFERENCE WORKING PAPER: A CHANGING GREAT LAKES ECONOMY: ECONOMIC AND ENVIRONMENTAL LINKAGES. Environment Canada and United States Environmental Protection Agency, 1994.

Allen, Robert. THE ILLUSTRATED NATURAL HISTORY OF CANADA: THE GREAT LAKES. Toronto: McClelland and Stewart, 1970.

ALTERNATIVES: PERSPECTIVES ON SOCIETY, TECHNOLOGY AND ENVIRONMENT. Special Issue. Saving the Great Lakes. Vol. 13, No. 3, September/October, 1986.

American Museum of Natural History. THE ENDURING GREAT LAKES. J. Rousmaniere (ed.). New York: W.W. Norton and Co., 1980.

Ashworth, William. THE LATE, GREAT LAKES. New York: Knopf, 1986.

Burns, Noel M. ERIE: THE LAKE THAT SURVIVED. Totowa, New Jersey: Rowman and Allanheld Publ., 1985.

Egerton, Frank N. OVERFISHING OR POLLUTION? CASE HISTORY OF A CONTROVERSY ON THE GREAT LAKES. Great Lakes Fishery Commission, Technical Report No. 41, Ann Arbor, Michigan, 1985.

Eichenlaub, Val. WEATHER AND CLIMATE OF THE GREAT LAKES BASIN. Notre Dame, Indiana: University of Notre Dame Press, 1979.

Eisenreich, S.J., C.J. Holland and T.C. Johnson. ATMOSPHERIC POLLUTANTS IN NATURAL WATER SYSTEMS. Ann Arbor, Michigan: Ann Arbor Science Publishers, 1980.

Ellis, W.D. LAND OF THE INLAND SEAS: THE HISTORIC AND BEAUTIFUL GREAT LAKES COUNTRY. Palo Alto: American West Publishing Co., 1974.

Emery, Lee. REVIEW OF FISH SPECIES INTRODUCED INTO THE GREAT LAKES, 1819-1974. Great Lakes Fishery Commission, Technical Report No. 45, Ann Arbor, Michigan, 1985.

Environment Canada. GREAT LAKES CLIMATOLOGICAL ATLAS. Saulesleja, A. (ed.). Atmospheric Environment Service. Ottawa: Canadian Government Publications Centre. (Cat. No. EN56-70/1986), 1986.

Environment Canada and United States Environmental Protection Agency. STATE OF THE LAKES ECOSYSTEM REPORT. July, 1995.

Federal Reserve Bank of Chicago and the Great Lakes Commission. THE GREAT LAKES ECONOMY: LOOKING NORTH AND SOUTH. Chicago, 1991.

Government of Canada. CURRENTS OF CHANGE; FINAL REPORT OF THE INQUIRY ON FEDERAL WATER POLICY. Ottawa: Supply and Services Canada, 1985.

Government of Canada. TOXIC CHEMICALS IN THE GREAT LAKES AND ASSOCIATED EFFECTS: SYNOPSIS, VOLUME 2, VOLUME 3. Ottawa: Supply and Services Canada, 1991.

Government of Quebec, St. Lawrence Development Secretariat. THE ST. LAWRENCE: A VITAL NATIONAL RESOURCE. Quebec, P.Q., 1985.

Great Lakes Basin Commission. GREAT LAKES BASIN COMMISSION FRAMEWORK STUDY. Public Information Office, Great Lakes Basin Commission, Ann Arbor, Michigan, 1976.

Great Lakes Fishery Commission. REHABILITATING GREAT LAKES ECOSYSTEMS. G.R. Francis et al. (eds). Technical Report No. 37, Ann Arbor, Michigan, 1979.

Great Lakes Fishery Commission. STRATEGIC VISION OF THE GREAT LAKES FISHERY COMMISSION FOR THE DECADE OF THE 1990S. Ann Arbor, Michigan, 1992.

Hartig, J., and N. Law. PROGRESS IN GREAT LAKES REMEDIAL ACTION PLANS: IMPLEMENTING THE ECOSYSTEM APPROACH IN GREAT LAKES AREAS OF CONCERN. Detroit: Wayne State University, 1994.

Health and Welfare Canada. HAVING YOUR CATCH AND EATING IT TOO: A FEW WORDS ABOUT SPORT FISH AND YOUR HEALTH. Great Lakes Health Effects Program. Ottawa: Supply and Services Canada, 1992.

Health and Welfare Canada. A VITAL LINK: HEALTH AND THE ENVIRONMENT IN CANADA. Ottawa: Supply and Services Canada, 1992.

Hough, J.L. THE GEOLOGY OF THE GREAT LAKES. University of Illinois Press, 1958.

International Joint Commission. AN ENVIRONMENTAL MANAGEMENT STRATEGY FOR THE GREAT LAKES SYSTEM. Final Report, International Reference Group on Great Lakes Pollution from Land Use Activities (PLUARG). Windsor, Ontario, 1978.

International Joint Commission. GREAT LAKES DIVERSIONS AND CONSUMPTIVE USES. Report by the International Great Lakes Diversion and Consumptive Uses Study Board, 1981.

International Joint Commission. REPORT ON GREAT LAKES WATER QUALITY. Report of the Great Lakes Water Quality Board. Presented at Kingston, Ontario, 1985.

International Joint Commission. REVISED GREAT LAKES WATER QUALITY AGREEMENT OF 1978 AS AMENDED BY PROTOCOL SIGNED NOVEMBER 18, 1987.

Jacobsen, Joseph L. "Prenatal Exposure to an Environmental Toxin: A Test of Multiple Effects", DEVELOPMENTAL PSYCHOLOGY, Vol. 20, No. 4, 1984.

Keating, Michael. TO THE LAST DROP: CANADA AND THE WORLD'S WATER CRISIS. Toronto: Macmillan of Canada, 1986.

Koonce, J. STATE OF THE LAKES ECOSYSTEM CONFERENCE WORKING PAPER: AQUATIC COMMUNITY HEALTH OF THE GREAT LAKES. Environment Canada and United States Environmental Protection Agency, 1994.

Kuchenberg, Tom. REFLECTIONS IN A TARNISHED MIRROR: THE USE AND ABUSE OF THE GREAT LAKES. Sturgeon Bay, Wisconsin: Golden Glow Publishing, 1978.

Le Strang, Jacques (ed.). THE GREAT LAKES - ST. LAWRENCE SYSTEM. Boyne City, Michigan: Harbor House Publishers Seaway Review, 1985.

J. Manno, et al. STATE OF THE LAKES ECOSYSTEM CONFERENCE WORKING PAPER: EFFECTS OF GREAT LAKES BASIN ENVIRONMENTAL CONTAMINANTS ON HUMAN HEALTH. Environment Canada and United States Environmental Protection Agency, 1994.

Marine Advisory Service of the Michigan Sea Grant College Program. LAKE SUPERIOR, MICHIGAN, HURON, ERIE, ONTARIO AND GREAT LAKES BASIN. Extension Bulletins E-1866 - 1871. Cooperative Extension Service, Michigan State University, East Lansing, Michigan, 1993.

Neilson, M., et al. STATE OF THE LAKES ECOSYSTEM CONFERENCE WORKING PAPER: NUTRIENTS: TRENDS AND SYSTEM RESPONSE. Environment Canada and United States Environmental Protection Agency, 1994.

Nriagu, J.A., and M.S. Simmons (eds). TOXIC CONTAMINANTS IN THE GREAT LAKES. New York: John Wiley and Sons, 1984.

Phillips, D.W., and J.A.W. McCulloch. THE CLIMATE OF THE GREAT LAKES BASIN. Toronto: Environment Canada, 1972.

Royal Commission on the Future of the Toronto Waterfront. REGENERATION: TORONTO'S WATERFRONT AND THE SUSTAINABLE CITY: FINAL REPORT. Ottawa: Supply and Services Canada, 1992.

Scott, S., R. Vezina and M. Webb. THE ST. LAWRENCE RIVER: ITS ECONOMY AND ENVIRONMENT. Toronto: The Centre For The Great Lakes Foundation, 1989.

The Nature Conservancy. THE CONSERVATION OF BIOLOGICAL DIVERSITY IN THE GREAT LAKES ECOSYSTEM: ISSUES AND OPPORTUNITIES. Chicago, Illinois, 1994.

TREATY BETWEEN THE UNITED STATES OF AMERICA AND GREAT BRITAIN RELATING TO BOUNDARY WATERS BETWEEN THE UNITED STATES AND CANADA. January 11, 1909.

University of Michigan. JOURNAL OF GREAT LAKES RESEARCH. All volumes. Ann Arbor, Michigan.

Wilson, E. O. THE DIVERSITY OF LIFE. New York: W.W. Norton and Company, 1992.

World Commission on Environment and Development. OUR COMMON FUTURE. Oxford University Press, 1987.

Sources for Maps and Photographic Credits

RELIEF, DRAINAGE AND URBAN AREAS (Page 2)

Canada, map, 1/5,000,000. Ottawa: Surveys and Mapping Branch, EMR, 1983.

Great Lakes Water Use, map, 1/1,584,000. Burlington: Inland Waters Directorate (Ontario Region), Environment Canada, 1980.

International Map of the World, map series, 1/1,000,000, sheets NL-17, NL-18, NM-15, NM-16. Ottawa: Surveys and Mapping Branch, EMR, various dates. International Map of the World, map series, 1/1,000,000 sheets NK-16, NK-17, NK-18, NL-15, NL-16. Washington: USGS, Department of the Interior, various dates.

Karta Mira, map series, 1/2,500,000, sheets 31, 32, 47, 48. Budapest: National Office of Lands and Mapping, various dates.

United States, map, 1/2,500,000, east sheet. Washington: USGS, Department of the Interior, 1972.

GEOLOGY AND MINERAL RESOURCES (Page 6)

Douglas, R.J.W. Geology and Economic Minerals of Canada, Part B. Ottawa: Geological Survey of Canada, EMR, 1976.

Geologic Map of North America, 1/1,000,000. Washington: USGS, Department of the Interior, 1965.

Glacial Map of the United States West of the Rocky Mountains, 1/1,750,000. New York: Geological Society of America, 1959.

Hough, J.L. Geology of the Great Lakes. Urbana: University of Illinois Press, 1958.

International Reference Group on Great Lakes Pollution from Land Use Activities, Inventory of Land Use and Land Use Practices in the United States Great Lakes Basin, Vol. 1. Windsor: IJC, 1976.

National Atlas of Canada, 4th ed. Ottawa: Surveys and Mapping Branch, EMR, 1973.

National Atlas of Canada, 5th ed. Ottawa: Surveys and Mapping Branch, EMR, 1978 and later.

National Atlas of the United States. Washington: USGS, Department of the Interior, 1970 and later.

Williams, H.R. Department of Geological Sciences, Brock University, St. Catharines, personal communication, 1986.

CLIMATE MAPS (Page 8)

Climatic Atlas Climatique - Canada, Map Series 1 - Temperature and Degree Days. Toronto: AES, Environment Canada, 1984.

Climatic Atlas of North and Central America, Vol. 1, Maps of Mean Temperature and Precipitation. Geneva: World Meteorological Organization, 1979.

Eichenlaub, Val L. Weather and Climate of the Great Lakes Basin. Notre Dame: University of Notre Dame Press, 1979.

Mudrey, D. AES, Environment Canada, Ottawa, personal communication, 1986.

Phillips, D.W., and J.A.W. McCulloch. The Climate of the Great Lakes Basin, Climatological Studies No. 20. Toronto: AES, Environment Canada, 1972.

Saulesleja, A. (ed.). Great Lakes Climatological Atlas. Toronto: AES, Environment Canada, 1986.

Shaw, A.B. Department of Geography, Brock University, St. Catharines, personal communication, 1986.

THE GREAT LAKES WATER SYSTEM (Page 10)

Great Lakes Diversion and Consumptive Uses. Windsor: IJC, 1985.

NFB Canada Map, no scale. Montreal: National Film Board of Canada, 1984.

HISTORICAL MAP (Page 16)

Transparency courtesy of National Archives of Canada, Ottawa.

LAND USE, FISHERIES AND EROSION (Page 19)

Great Lakes Fishery Commission, 1991.

NOAA - AVHRR Land Cover, Manitoba Centre For Remote Sensing, 1991.

Stewart, Chris. Canadian Hydrographic Service, personal communication, 1992.

Tilt, John. Ontario Ministry of Natural Resources, personal communication, 1992.

WATERBORNE COMMERCE (Page 21)

Coastwise Shipping Statistics 1990. Ottawa: Statistics Canada, 1992.

International Seaborne Shipping Port Statistics 1990. Ottawa: Statistics Canada, 1992.

St. Lawrence Seaway Traffic Report for 1990. Navigation Season. Ottawa St. Lawrence Seaway Authority, 1992.

Waterborne Commerce of the United States, Calendar Year 1990, Part 3 - Waterways and Harbors Great Lakes. Washington Corps of Engineers, Department of the Army, 1992.

RECREATION AND SPORTS (Page 23)

Annual Meeting of the Great Lakes Fishery Commission. Appendix XXXII. Ann Arbor, 1986,

Dean, W.G. (ed.). Economic Atlas of Ontario. Toronto: University of Toronto Press, 1969.

Illinois, Indiana, Michigan, Minnesota, New York, Ohio, Pennsylvania, Wisconsin road maps, various scales. Chicago: Rand McNally & Co., 1986.

Miscellaneous tourist pamphlets and brochures for Ontario and the states within the Great Lakes basin.

Ontario road map 1/800,000 and 1/1,600,000. Toronto: Ontario Ministry of Recreation and Tourism, 1993.

Shore Use and Erosion Work Group, Great Lakes Basin Framework Study, Appendix R9, Recreational Boating. Ann Arbor: Great Lakes Basin Commission, 1975.

The National Atlas of the United States. Washington: USGS, Department of the Interior, 1970 and later.

EMPLOYMENT AND INDUSTRIAL STRUCTURE (Page 25)

1990 Census of Population, Vol. 1, Characteristics of the Population, Chap. C, General Social and Economic Characteristics, Parts 15, 16, 24, 25, 34, 37, 40 and 51. Washington: Bureau of the Census, U.S. Department of Commerce, 1991.

1991 Census of Canada, Population, Economic Characteristics, Ontario. Ottawa: Statistics Canada, 1992.

1991 Census of Canada. Reference Maps. Census Divisions and Subdivisions. Ottawa: Statistics Canada, 1991.

TRANSPORTATION AND ENERGY MAPS (Page 26)

Generating Station December Installed Capacity. Toronto: Ontario Hydro, 1985. mimeo.

Handy Railroad Atlas of the United States. Chicago: Rand McNally & Co., 1982.

Illinois, Indiana, Michigan, Minnesota, New York, Ohio, Pennsylvania, Wisconsin road maps, various scales. Chicago: Rand McNally & Co., 1986.

Inventory of Power Plants in the United States 1985. Washington: Energy Information Administration, U.S. Department of Energy, 1986.

National Atlas of Canada, 5th ed. Ottawa: Surveys and Mapping Branch, EMR, 1978 and later.

Ontario, road map, 1/800,000 and 1/1,600,000. Toronto: Ontario Ministry of Transportation and Communications, 1986.

Sectional Aeronautical Charts, map series, 1/500,000, Chicago, Detroit, Green Bay and Lake Huron sheets. Washington: U.S. Department of Commerce, 1986.

The Gifts of Nature. Toronto: Ontario Hydro, 1979.

National Atlas of the United States. Washington: United States Geological Survey, Department of the Interior, 1970 and later.

VIA Rail pamphlets.

DISTRIBUTION OF POPULATION (Page 28)

1980 Census of Population, Vol. 1, Characteristics of the Population, Chap. C, General Social and Economic Characteristics, Parts 15, 16, 24, 25, 34, 37, 40 and 51. Washington: Bureau of the Census, U.S. Department of Commerce, 1983.

1981 Census of Canada, Population etc., Selected Characteristics, Ontario. Ottawa: Statistics Canada, 1982.

STATE OF THE LAKES (Page 34)

An Atlas of Contaminants in Eggs of Fish-Eating Colonial Birds of the Great Lakes (1970-1988 and 1989-1992), Vol. I and Vol. II. Environment Canada, Canadian Wildlife Service.

Government of Canada. Toxic Chemicals in the Great Lakes and Associated Effects: Vol. I and Vol. II. Ottawa: Supply and Services Canada, 1991.

Neilson, M., et al. State of the Lakes Ecosystem Conference Working paper: Nutrients: Trends and System Response. Environment Canada and United States Environmental Protection Agency, 1994.

ECOREGIONS, DRAINAGE BASINS AND WETLANDS (Page 38)

Ecodistricts of Southern Canada, draft maps, 1/2,000,000, no date.

Ecoregions of the coterminous United States, maps, 1:7,500,000 by James Omernik, Corvallis Environmental Research Laboratories, U.S. EPA, 1994.

International Reference Group on Great Lakes Pollution from Land Use Activities, Inventory of Land Use and Land Use Practices in the Canadian Great Lakes Basin, Vol. 1. Windsor: International Joint Commission, 1977.

Rubec, C. Lands Directorate, Environment Canada, Ottawa, personal communication, 1986.

Shore Use and Erosion Work Group, Great Lakes Basin Framework Study, Appendix 10, Power. Ann Arbor: Great Lakes Basin Commission, 1975.

Wickware, G., Hunter and Associates, Mississauga, personal communication, 1987.

PHOTOGRAPHIC CREDITS

Pages 3, 7, 9, 11 (left and right) and 12: D. Cowell, Geomatics International, Burlington, Ontario.

Pages 5 (left), 29 and 31 (left and right): Great Lakes Program Office, U.S. EPA, Chicago, Illinois.

Page 5 (right): Harold Murphy, Hamilton Harbour RAP Office, Burlington, Ontario.

Pages 11 (center), 20 (left), 22 (left) and 40: CCIW, Burlington, Ontario.

Pages 13, 43: U.S. National Parks Service, Indiana Dunes National Lakeshore.

Page 14 (left): University of Wisconsin, Extension Service.

Pages 14 (right), 42: Earth Images Foundation, St. Catharines, Ontario.

Page 16: National Archives of Canada, NMC-6411, Ottawa, Ontario.

Page 17: Royal Ontario Museum, Toronto, Ontario.

Page 20 (right): Great Lakes Commission, Ann Arbor, Michigan.

Page 22 (right): Great Lakes Health Effects Program, Environmental Health Directorate, Health Canada, Ottawa, Ontario.

Page 24 (top): Peter J. Schulz, Chicago, Illinois.

Page 24 (bottom): Metropolitan Toronto Convention and Visitors Association, Toronto, Ontario.

Page 30: Lake Michigan Federation, Chicago, Illinois.

Page 35: J. Lubner, Wisconsin Sea Grant, Milwaukee, Wisconsin.

Page 39: Little River Enhancement Group, Windsor, Ontario.

Page 41: P. Bertram, Great Lakes National Program Office, U.S. EPA, Chicago Illinois.

PRODUCTION

Computerized mapping and map artwork by Geomatics International and Rawlings Communications, Burlington, Ontario (5 pages). All other maps by Brock University Cartography.

Design, layout and artwork for text and front cover by Agensky and Company Limited, Toronto, Ontario.

Copy editing by Leon Smith, Ajax, Ontario, and Robyn Packard, Thornhill, Ontario.